Reflections on Faith

Thoughts and Devotions

Ronnie Worsham

ISBN: 1533655499
ISBN 13: 9781533655493

To my brothers and sisters:
Dean, Don, Judy, Tom, Jane, Joy, and Jack, my lifelong heroes,
who have loved me, believed in me, guided me, and gone ahead
of me in this walk of faith we have lived out together as family.

Table of Contents

Introduction:

A Personal Message from the Author

Faith is not something that can be had on a moment's notice. Faith is not a mere belief that something is or exists. Faith is trust, and not just the trust that something is or that we ought to believe in it or rely on it. Biblical faith is the whole-person experience of coming to believe in God, determining him to be real and reliable, and subsequently, making a commitment to serve and rely on him.

Faith is not only the experience of a moment, but more so, it is an experience of a lifetime. It is something that grows over time. It is an embryo that germinates within us from small seeds of truth into a whole-life belief system that transforms the believer. A few seeds of faith will produce a whole harvest—a harvest of righteousness. Biblical faith will encompass all of our thinking and our lifestyle; it will never remain only an inner notion that fails to express itself in our identity and essence.

Our faith—our beliefs about God, the world, ourselves, and others—is the operating system of the thought processes that determine what our moment-to-moment behaviors will be—*from the overflow of the heart, the mouth speaks.* These collective behaviors constitute our lifestyles—who we are, what we are, what we do, and what we are becoming. A flawed belief system will produce flawed behaviors and flawed lives. There is no avoiding it. To fix a life, one must fix the faith behind it—*clean the inside of the cup, and the outside will be clean as well.*

Our salvation—our being on right terms with God—is based on our faith; not faith in and of ourselves though, but faith in God. It is based on our belief in *his* grace and goodness and not on anything of ourselves. Salvation is about our ongoing relationship with God, and therefore, is not about a single "faith moment" or some fleeting, momentary experience. It is not like joining a club or attending a college and taking on the identity of a mascot or wearing a logo tee shirt. A relationship with God is a defining, lifetime experience that becomes an eternal one—*we are not of those who shrink back and are destroyed but of those who believe and are saved.* Salvation is about our acceptance of what reality actually is—that God exists and that he is in control of this world that often seems out of control. And that Jesus Christ is Lord and our only avenue of access to this saving reality. It is a faith that is not to be burdensome but only to bring us the blessings of living out the truth of a glorious God.

Faith, however, is not easy—*this is the work God requires of you.* In a fallen world full of deception and falsity, humanity quickly adapts, and thus, we put up our guards and in actuality trust very little. We are constantly bombarded with information of all kinds, coming at us from all directions, aimed at igniting emotions in us that will motivate us to go or do or buy or be, all based on the ambitions and desires of others. Little to nothing is really sent our way that is solely to give us something or to help us. We are swamped by marketing and hype—advertisements, phone calls, e-mails, and even knocks on our doors.

In all honesty, indeed, little *can* be completely trusted in this corrupted age. In this ever-changing and often seemingly crazy world, little can be relied on. Nothing and no one has the control to always be what is promised, intended, or wanted.

But if one can come to see the powerful entity behind it all—Yahweh, the Great I Am, the one who merely is—one finally finds the fixed, the immutable, the unchanging, the forever Existent One. We finally find the divine constant that can always be trusted—*every word of God proves true.* It is this faith that brings reliable hope, real expectation—*our hope does not disappoint us.*

This kind of faith, however, must be built on a foundation of reason, logic, and truth. Reasonable faith, biblical faith, must be built on a strong foundation, from the ground up—*like an expert builder I laid a foundation.* There is only one such foundation, and He is the solid rock of eternity who is immovable and completely reliable—*no one can lay any foundation other than the one already laid, which is Jesus Christ.*

This book is written from deep within the heart and soul of one who first came to truly know Christ forty-three years ago. In a storm of doubt and fear, as well as a time of social and personal upheaval, a twenty-one-year-old science major, sitting in a chemistry class, was inwardly stirred and spurred to try to see if there was truly something or someone behind this physical world he was intellectually studying to understand.

However, in the reflections herein, I write conversationally, neither as a learned scientist nor a biblical scholar, even though I've studied each field extensively. I write as a fellow sojourner, a struggler, a wonderer, and a seeker of truth. Herein, there is reason, and there is emotion; there is mind, and there is heart; there is logic, and there is intuition. It is sometimes written to explain, and it is sometimes written to inspire. Much is assumed. At times little explanation is given. Its purpose is to serve readers, for at least a time, as a perch, a vantage point, something to ponder, a rock to sun upon, a branch to light upon, and a park bench to sit on. It is intended to invite you, the reader, to sit still and think, not so much to do anything, but to allow your mind to be stretched and possibly your heart filled. Any positive change that might happen on the inside will automiatically bear its fruit outwardly.

I write out of a deep conviction that there is a great divine being behind this awesome creation, Yahweh, God, and, within his plan, all makes sense, because, in the greater scheme of things, it is most logical. Neither human scientific knowledge nor human philosophy, neither human psychology nor human theology are complete. Therefore none of them are completely reliable to answer the most basic human questions: Where did we come from? What are we doing here? What is our ultimate fate and destiny?

However, these disciplines of study and thought are at present the best we have available to us to think through the meaning and purpose of life. And in these quests for knowledge, for truth, and for understanding, I believe we can each find the necessary seeds to build the constructs that will, in turn, help us build reliable belief systems based on the basic truths to be found. I believe faith is not only possible; I believe it is probable when one merely seeks pure truth—*everyone on the side of truth comes to me [Christ]*.

I write out of the conviction that the Bible is inspired by God through his own ways and means—that over the early ages, he led certain people to write down what they saw, heard, experienced, or were taught by God or others. Its origin, construction, and preservation are nothing short of miraculous. I find it the most amazing book on life and faith. In it is found purpose, meaning, and hope. It leads the honest thinker, I believe, to awe and wonder. It provides help in times of need, answers in times of confusion and trouble, and instruction on life and relationships. It challenges us to look and think beyond our current visible reality. It troubles us and stirs us to awaken from our dull and selfish daze. It confronts us, in our own sinful condition, with its stories of often even worse sins. It does not elevate humanity; it rather humbles us by right-sizing us. It tells our truth, because it tells the truth. The humility that can be gained from it seems to be a rare commodity in an often proud world in desperate need of it!

I have long loved a poem by James Gray called, "The Bible." The third verse summarizes my conviction about the Bible with which the faith reflections contained in this book have been written.

Despised and torn in pieces,
By infidels decried,
With thunderbolts of hatred
The haughty cynics pride—
All these have railed against it
In this and other lands;
Yet dynasties have fallen,
And still the Bible stands!

The Bible is referred to and quoted often, and unless otherwise noted, all quotes are from the New International Version of the Bible, 2011.

So I invite you to walk with me on a journey of my own heart and soul and mind. I invite you to sit and ponder with me these thoughts and devotions on faith, as well as my inspirations, prayers, and reflections. I ask you not to read my book as a critic, a cynic, or an emotional or intellectual infant seeking baby food. I ask you to read it as a fellow struggler, as if sitting on a park bench next to another, taking a break from a long walk, another just like you, pondering together life and the divine.

I was called to be a disciple, an evangelist, a pastor, and a friend of fellow sinners about forty-three years ago from this writing. I have remained faithful to that calling all these years, through many trials and challenges, likely, for the most part, brought on by my own weakness and ineptitude. I have also experienced great blessings along the way, and in my later years, I am now living the dream God began laying on my heart over four decades ago, as I pondered long and hard what I believe truth, knowledge, existence, and our purpose to be. In my own personal quest for truth, I found Jesus Christ behind all knowledge and beyond the big bang. He had always been there.

So, scientifically, practically, and theologically, to quote the apostle Paul, this is *my gospel*, because Christ is my gospel (Rom. 2:16; 2 Tim. 2:8).

Ronnie Worsham

1

Doubt Is the Water Faith Walks On

Where there is faith, there is doubt, for, "We live by faith and not by sight."[1] One man said to Jesus, "I do believe; help me overcome my unbelief!"[2] Or restated, "I believe, but I need help resolving my doubt." What we call "knowledge" is really only what we believe to be true with the most certainty. Humans can always be wrong, thus absolute knowing is only an illusion. All we hold as truth is always finally dependent on faith.

What we humans call "miracles" or the "supernatural" might only reflect a deeper understanding of natural law, such as humans developing the ability to fly. Or it could, in fact, constitute an intervention of God overruling natural law, such as Jesus raising the dead man, Lazarus.[3] That something appears "unbelievable" does not at all mean it is not true or did not happen. Also that something appears absolutely true does not therefore make it so. The Bible asserts without any equivocation that the "unbelievable" occurred numerous times in revealing the power and work of God. Jesus is the ultimate revelation of God, and therefore, he did things only God could do.

Matthew, Mark, and John all record for us an incident in which Jesus came walking on the water toward the apostles' boat one night, out on the Sea of Galilee. Peter and the others were of course frightened, and doubting that it was Jesus, they surmised it was perhaps a ghost. Peter said to him, "Lord, if it's you, tell me to come to you on the water." Jesus said, "Come." Matthew's account tells us,

> Then Peter got down out of the boat, walked on the water, and came toward Jesus. But when he saw the wind, he was afraid and, beginning to sink, cried out, "Lord, save me!" Immediately Jesus reached out his hand and caught him. "You of little faith," he said, "why did you doubt?"[4]

Of course Peter doubted! This was a grown man who found it easier to believe that a ghost was coming toward them on the water than to believe an amazing man, Jesus, was walking on water. Of course he doubted it was Jesus because he had never seen any-body walk on water! He had never heard of anybody walking on water. But in that moment, he apparently somewhat believed, or at least wondered if, Jesus could make him walk on water. That is, if indeed, it was Jesus who was approaching them. However, he didn't maintain for very long his belief, at least with any great degree of certainty, and thus, he began to sink when he became afraid. He at first walked on the water when his faith overcame his doubt. He then sank when his doubt overcame his faith.

All of humanity lives by faith in all sorts of things. That is, we believe things we live by with a high degree of certainty. Time, per-sonal experience, experimentation, and repetition can serve to increase or decrease that degree of certainty but never fully and unequivocally prove anything. Even in such disciplines as mathe-matics where "proofs" are offered, most of us have to trust those who devised the proof, as we cannot fully understand what was done to prove it and how it proved anything. We can always be wrong. There can always be exceptions to what is held as truth. And we know it.

True biblical faith is based on reason and evidence. It is based on thousands of years of history and tradition. "Now faith is con-fidence in what we hope for and assurance about what we do not see."[5] Biblically, hope is expectation, and its certainty is propor-tional to the faith or trust involved. We expect things to happen in proportion to our trust or belief in whomever or whatever led us to expect something in the first place.

Many, indeed, have blind faith in religion. Of course they do. So much ignorance, superstition, and falsehood are justified by religion. Various groups, even religious ones, are formed to investigate all sorts of paranormal things—ghosts and hauntings, UFOs, health hoaxes, and such, but blind faith also operates in science and philosophy as well. Such faith is based on what some people want to believe, not on an honest pursuit of truth. Hypotheses and theories are examples of science's beliefs. Often studies of all kinds are merely attempts to prove what is already believed more than to discover what the truth really is. Academia does not call what it believes "faith," because many in the intellectual community see faith as blind by definition. It is instead called "reason." At best however, it is only reasonable faith. And, what many in religion call faith is mere feeling and is not very reasoned at all. In reality, honest faith and fair reasoning should never be in conflict with each other. They should harmonize and balance each other out. Faith is just as essential to reason as reason is to faith.

Real faith—strong faith—has certainty to it that is based on evidence and reason. It is honest and it is fair. It is merely seeking to discover the truth, not to fabricate it. Blind faith is weak faith, emotional faith; it is impotent faith. And biased beliefs motivated by personal agendas, but masquerading as reason, constitute the blindest faith of all.

There are reasons to believe in God. There are reasons to believe in the Bible. There are reasons to believe Christ is the Son of God. Just as there are reasons to believe in the big bang theory of cosmic origin. And there are reasons to believe dinosaurs existed. There is evidence, but none of us living at present witnessed any of it. Our beliefs are based on evidence, be that evidence strong or weak. We say we "know" things as an expression of the higher degree of certainty with which we believe them; that is, we see their existence as beyond a reasonable doubt.

And we can be assured that every day, we must live our lives according to faith. Everyone lives by faith, faith in something or someone. We have no other choice.

Inspiration: Humankind had long dreamed of being able to fly. Some had experiemented and tried. Then the Wright brothers and others showed the world that it was possible through mechanical means. Thousands now soar through the air daily, from one place to another, and at speeds once unimaginable. Some even fly into outer space. Similarly, many in the field of sports thought it impossible for humans to run a mile in four minutes or less. However, in 1954, Roger Bannister accomplished the feat. Then, six weeks later, another broke that record. Just over a year later, three others ran sub-four-minute miles in one race! History is full of other examples of the things humans have long doubted but that faith made reality. Granted, faith can indeed be misguided and blind, but faith itself is not a bad thing; faith is a good thing—an essential thing—when based on evidence and reason. And every single human lives by it, whether we want to admit it or not. Thus, we need to be in charge of our faith, rather than just let it happen via ignorance or bias. We need to choose our faith carefully and wisely, for our faith is what allows us to rise above doubt in our quest for the truth of what is truly possible for us. Faith allows us to plunge into the deep waters of the seemingly impossible and resurface with gold nuggets of possibility. Faith allows us to fly and run fast. Doubt must not deter our faith, but it must only hone and purify it. Doubt truly is the water that our faith walks on, and it is the air that our faith soars through, as well.

Prayer: Father, I do believe. Help me today with my unbelief. Lead me to honestly seek pure truth and to develop what I believe based on reasons, not simply what I want to believe. Help me to be honest and sincere. Help me to be fair and compassionate. And help me to stand on the side of truth, whatever that truth might be.

Reflection: How have I begun walking on the water of doubt in the way of Jesus and then begun to sink because my doubt and fear overcame my faith? What are the benefits I have experienced due to my faith in God or anyone or anything else for that matter?

References:
1. 2 Cor. 5:7.
2. Mark 9:24.
3. John 11:43.
4. Matthew 14:22-36; Mark 14:45-56; John 6:16-24.
5. Heb. 11:1.

2

If There Is a Mother Nature, She Sure Has an Intelligent Father

In the Old Testament, a "fool" was the one who disregarded or disbelieved in God.[1] The apostle Paul agreed, saying,

> What may be known about God is plain to them, because God has made it plain to them. For since the creation of the world, God's invisible qualities—his eternal power and divine nature—have been clearly seen, being understood from what has been made, so that people are without excuse.[2]

The New Testament thus considers unbelief inexcusable. Unbelievers in God are "without excuse." That's the way scriptures see it, period.

God's eternal power and divine nature are clearly seen when we look at what has been made. It is, in the words of Paul, inexcusable to deny or ignore it. The book of Hebrews asserts, "And without faith, it is impossible to please God, because anyone who comes to him must believe that he exists and that he rewards those who earnestly seek him."[3] From the Bible's point of view, to deny God is to deny the foundational, universal truth. It is, in fact, to disregard reality.

Both religion and science have drawn the wrong kinds of boundaries around their disciplines. Religion, or faith, has long tried to force on humanity certain scientific beliefs based on seemingly a priori assumptions of knowledge. Such ideas are assumed bits of knowledge that come before any honest, objective observations, study, and experience of the universe. More often than not the perpetuation of such beliefs is the result of the handing down of religious, family, and social beliefs and traditions.

As an example, at one time, the church officially, and obviously wrongfully, taught that the earth was the center of the universe, and to believe otherwise was considered heresy. Galileo was officially convicted of heresy in 1633 by the Roman Catholic Inquisition for his support of the modern scientific view of heliocentrism (that the sun and not the earth is the center of the solar system).

However, the church was only clinging to what was considered the scientific convention of the time, as did most of the great scientists, philosophers, and thinkers of the day. Everybody simply "knew" it to be fact. However, it was not fact. It was not reality, even though great thinkers believed it to be. The church was not anti-science as many may assume. It was partnered with science, which also operates by its own models of faith, and thus the church at the time believed in the geocentric model (that the earth was the center of the solar system). Based on traditional views of faith and scripture, and even with no actual scripture that necessitated such a view, the church initially strongly refused to consider any later observations from science that clearly disputed the original view—or the generally held belief of science of the time. The church at large has continued to often be the last institution to acknowledge clear evidence contrary to previously held views, often defending positions that are unnecessary and untenable. True faith accepts that it must continue to grow by reviewing and upgrading foundational views and their corollaries. Faith that refuses to grow is already dead.

Modern science, on the other hand, generally assumes a priori that everything originates from the physical, including all things otherwise considered "spiritual" or metaphysical. Since science, by its very nature, studies the physical, it must exclude any empirical consideration of anything else, such as the spiritual. Science in fact does not have the tools or expertise to even address what might be non-material or spiritual. When either discipline tries to impose itself on the other rather than learning from each other, incomplete or inaccurate conclusions follow. Religion opposed to science is unwise and ignorant; science opposed to religion is foolish and narrow-minded.

Rather than including knowledge and information from one another, in an equal partnership, which takes into consideration both the revelation of the creation and the revelation of scripture, both science and religion each often unnecessarily seem to set itself up as the one and only supreme determiner of truth. Simple, pure truth should be what we all honestly and sincerely seek, regardless of where it is to be found. In a most powerful claim, Jesus stated that all who seek truth ultimately come to believe in and listen to him.[4]

As has been pointed out, Paul clearly states that creation itself is a revelation from God through which we can perceive the Creator's eternal power and divine nature. In other words, we should be able to clearly see that the divine is real, that the spiritual exists—eternity is bound up in it, and that the visible world emanates from the unseen, eternal one. We can even learn about the personal attributes of this divinity through what has been created and how it operates.

While creation reveals God's existence, divine nature, and eternal power, scripture more fully explains God. It explains what we see and experience. In fact, scripture says that Jesus was the exact representation of God's being.[5] Thus, the two disciplines of religion and science should be equal partners in seeking out the truth of origins, existence, and purpose, rather than seeking to "Lord it over" one another. Science studies the creation, which shows us God exists and displays to us his eternal power and divine nature, and the other delves into scripture and the wisdom of the ages, helping us understand our spiritual nature and God's plan and will for this world he created.

Scripture asserts, "He has made everything beautiful in its time. He has also set eternity in the human heart; yet no one can fathom what God has done from beginning to end."[6] Anthropology and archeology have found humanity to have believed in the divine from the earliest times. Yes, atheism has apparently long existed, but throughout the ages, studies and surveys indicate the vast majority of humans have believed in, and still believe in, the divine and in an afterlife of some kind. Scripture says it is imprinted on our hearts.[7]

All should therefore carefully consider both the spiritual and the physical in our lives. These are not two different things; they are two facets of the same thing—our existence. Therefore, all of us must, to some degree, be both theologian *and* scientist. Theology often overanalyzes the ambiguous to the neglect of the obvious. Science often overanalyzes the obvious to the neglect of the humanly ambiguous. The reality is, they need each other. One without the other is deficient and even dangerous. They are not mutually exclusive, but rather they are mutually essential in the whole honest human experience of truth.

Inspiration: Albert Einstein once said, "Concepts that have proven useful in ordering things easily achieve such authority over us that we forget their earthly origins and accept them as unalterable givens." The human reality is that, generally, people believe what they are taught growing up—our traditions, even though we all see clear evidence that in every society beliefs are handed down that are patently misguided or even untrue. Also, it is all-too-easy for any of us to believe mistruths and misinformation if enough people believe them. It matters not if it involves religion, science, philosophy, politics, and so forth. For example, as previously noted, for centuries it was held that the earth was the center of the universe. It was universally and by convention believed so strongly that the Catholic Church held it as a part of church doctrine. It had seemed to prove sensible in human understanding of the universe. But it was incorrect. Emerging science then proved this scientifically, socially, and religiously held belief to be incorrect. The reality is that the belief had come from science itself and was assumed to be true by everyone else including the church! But it should never have been a core doctrinal concern of religion in the first place.

On the other hand, in the fourteenth century, the bubonic plague started in Asia and spread into Russia, Europe, and Africa. Some reports claim that up to a third of the world's population, some sixty million people, died in the epidemic. Before an understanding of the role of germs in causing and spreading diseases became clear, a Jewish physician and student of the Old Testament saw that filth and refuse were a likely cause of, or at least associated with, the disease, and in the Jewish ghettos, he led a cleanup campaign using Old Testament hygiene instructions. The plague in the Jewish ghettos was only 5 percent of what it was in other areas, which also unfortunatly led to accusations that the Jews were somehow causing the disease elsewhere! This health lesson helped lay a foundation for modern germ theory and the treatment, alleviation, and prevention of many horrendous diseases. Ultimately, it was not science and medicine that revealed the real cause of the bubonic plague pandemic—it was faith and religion, stemming from the ancient writings of scripture. There are plenty of other examples of the positive effects of sound and reasonable faith on social, psychological, and physical health and well-being. And similarly there are plenty of examples of the positive effects on faith and religion of science and other secular fields. The reality is that a separation of science and faith is at best an ambiguous one, and at worst it is imaginary.

Prayer: Today, help us, Lord, to perceive you through what you have made. Help us see your reality—your intelligence, your artistry, your engineering, your architecture, your love, and your gracefulness. Help us also understand you in what you have revealed through scripture and through Jesus Christ—your purposefulness, your design for creation, your plans for humankind, your love for us, your goodness, your kindness, and your mercy for us. May our knowledge and our perceptions merge into a whole glorious experience of all you intended for us from the beginning. Help us to recognize you, to know you, to see you in the creation you made, and to experience you daily in a real and profound way.

Reflection: What about my knowledge of science and creation leads me most to believe in God, and what about it causes me doubt? How might I better hone my search for the truth? How will recognizing God in creation help me to grow in my experience of him?

References:
1. Ps. 14:1.
2. Rom. 1:19–20.
3. Heb. 11:6.
4. John 18:37.
5. Heb. 1:3.
6. Eccles. 3:11.
7. Rom. 2:15.

3

Subjectivity Is a Mortal Enemy of Truth

Subjectivity is a scourge of humanity. It is a mortal enemy of faith and a right perception of truth. At best, subjectivity skews the truth, and at worst, it completely obliterates it. It drives each of us to interpret the world around us as being about "me." All roads lead to me. All situations must favor me, and if they do not, a wrong has occurred. All must make sense to my personal universal construct, whatever it may be. But subjectivity leads to falsehood. And falsehood is an enemy of humanity.

When we are babies, we are completely self-centered. The world perceptually revolves around us. We are mainly operating on instinct. The world is the bosom we feed on, the crib we lie in, and where we presently exist. The only needs that we perceive are our own—to eat when we feel the urge, to wake when we wake, to be upright when the urge hits, to lie down in response to some inner signal, to be comfortable, and never uncomfortable. "Right" is to be comforted. "Wrong" is to be discomforted. Sadly, some seem to never grow out of it. Many seem to only partially grow out of it. All of us must fight to completely shed this comfy insulation of infancy.

To be subjective is to interpret things from a personal perspective. Subjectivism places the emphases on one's own feelings, moods, perspectives, and attitudes. In philosophy, it is seen as relating to the way one experiences things in their own mind. Generally, it may be seen as thoughts or opinions based on feelings or opinions rather than facts.[1] Reality is seen as what is perceived, rather than something that is apart from the observer.

But when a temporal, finite being self-defines an eternal, infinite world around them, objective truth perishes. And there are only two real perspectives to be had—the observer's dependent perspective or an independent perspective from the outside: What is it all to me, or what am I to all of it?

It all goes back to the original two-tree choices in the Garden of Eden, as depicted in the Bible—the Tree of the Knowledge of Good and Evil and the Tree of Life. The fruit of the first represents self-reliance, self-determination, and independence. This perspective can be seen as coming from the perspective of the individual specifically, or from the common perspective of all humanity generally. Either way, it's subjectivity. The scripture says that to eat of it is to die. The second, the Tree of Life, represents reliance on the infinite, eternal God, and not on self—objectivity.[2]

Objectivity is viewing the world as being "based on facts rather than feelings or opinions; not influenced by feelings."[3] That which is objective is said to be that which exists outside of one's own mind, out in the real world. To be objective is to see reality as it actually is and not as we would have it be.

Objectively, the world all begins to make sense because we try to see the world in reality. If we subjectively try to interpret the world as revolving around us or being all about us, we most assuredly get everything wrong. This is because we are using the wrong starting point, the wrong reference point, and the wrong lens. The world existed long before we arrived and will likely exist long after we go. But if we define the world objectively, in an infinite perspective, independent of self, we have the basis for a real and right understanding of the universe—assuming we objectively find the right reference point for discovering truth outside of ourselves.

The only two honest choices, generally speaking, are and have always been humanism, "truth" as defined from a subjective, personal, human perspective, or theism, "truth" as based on an objective, impersonal perspective from without. There have always been only two choices. There are subcategories of the two, but only two primary categories, two choices from two perspectives—two trees, two roads, believing in self or believing in God or the divine. Jesus says the first tree and the broad road lead to death. It is the fare many eat and the road that many traverse. He explained that it is a narrow road that leads to life and only a few will travel down it.[4]

The "fool" disregards or says there is no God.[5] It is one thing for a newborn to be oblivious of Mom, Dad, and other caretakers, simply and instinctively demanding personal satisfaction and comfort. It is another thing completely, however, for a two- or three-year-old to deny the existence of others around them, and thus to continue demanding that the world revolve only around them, oblivious of the reality of others. For a kid to deny the existence and will of his parents is not wise and should bring on a properly administered "reality check." A child that is not taught an awareness of and sensitivity to others, especially their parents, will usually turn out to be a disturbed person. Listening to parents or guardians will keep a child out of a lot of trouble, away from significant dangers, and on a track to getting and doing what is good and healthy. To subjectively deny the existence of or to disregard the will of one's parents and to follow one's own inner instincts and impulses is, to a child, to eat of the fruit of the Tree of the Knowledge of Good and Evil. You're on your own, baby—not good. And it is in Jesus's words, "the road that leads to destruction." Trusting parents and guardians is eating the fruit of the Tree of Life and, is in Jesus's words, "the road that leads to life." Jesus is in the end the life.

In the Bible, it is the Antichrist that denies that Jesus is God in the flesh—the truth of God, the way of God to life, the eternal Word of God.[6] It is the Antichrist that will set himself up as God.[7] And it is the "anti-truth," the purely subjective, that is derived only from within oneself. Paul wrote of the ancients, whom he called "fools," and whom denied and departed from God,

> For although they knew God, they neither glorified him as God nor gave thanks to him, but their thinking became futile and their foolish hearts were darkened. Although they claimed to be wise, they became fools and exchanged the glory of the immortal God for images made to look like a mortal human being and birds and animals and reptiles. Therefore, God gave them over in the sinful desires of their hearts to sexual impurity for the degrading of their bodies with one another. They exchanged the truth about God for a lie, and worshiped and served created things rather than the Creator—who is forever praised… they did not think it worthwhile to retain the knowledge of God, so God gave them over to a depraved mind, so that they do what ought not to be done.[8]

Note, "their foolish hearts were darkened" and "they became fools." As already explained, in the Old Testament, a "fool" was one who disbelieved or disregarded God. The outcome of such is always tragic, as seen in the text subsequent to the previous quote from Romans.[9]

Subjectivity is our enemy, if we begin our thought processes with it, because it can lead us to believe what is not true or to not see reality as it is. It causes us to exchange the truth for a lie. It is a one-way look into a two-way mirror, in that we are not seeing through to what is on the other side, but are only seeing a reflection of ourselves. We are not seeing ahead, only behind. We are not seeing ourselves in respect to the fixed and eternal; we are seeing the fixed and eternal in respect to ourselves.

There is a place for subjectivity within the truth itself. We ultimately have to apply what is the objective truth to ourselves in a subjective way, asking such questions as: How does the objective truth apply to me as an individual? What are its implications to me? How do I feel about such and such? What do I like, or what do I prefer in things? What are my interests? What is in my best interest? Understood in its proper perspective to the objective world, our own personal, subjective perspective actually becomes a part of objective reality itself, regardless if it is indeed right or wrong, true or untrue. It is always real though.

Faith is only useful when we are trusting in what is real and true though. Faith in what is not real and is not true can only lead to destruction because we are not operating on the facts, as best as they can be determined. Living only subjectively, when we come to adolescence and adulthood, we try to continue to operate as a newborn. And we starve ourselves to death in what appears reasonable but in the larger perspective is irrational.

Salvation is not just by faith alone, because our faith can be in ourselves, others, and in things that are not true. Everyone must live by faith in something; therefore, everyone that lives by faith is not necessarily saved. Our salvation is by our faith exclusively in Christ Jesus.[10] Because he is the truth.[11] That "Jesus is Lord" is the ultimate conclusion of the whole Bible.[12] Objectivity concerning the identity of Christ is essential to those who would experience eternal life as God knows it, as objectivity is necessary for perceiving truth rightly. For getting Jesus, as the truth, rightly.

Inspiration: The human cell is an amazing thing—clearly, a design miracle. To explain cell development, in a gross oversimplification, every human cell within an individual is produced by the original zygote, the cell produced when a female egg cell combines with a male sperm cell. And there are more than two hundred cell types in the body that are ultimately produced from this first cell. Within just a few days, a newly formed zygote forms what is called a *blastocyst*, which is a ball of 150 to 200 cells. These cells then produce all the different cell types that function in the tissues, organs, and systems of a human body (cells make up tissues, e.g., stomach lining; tissues make up organs, e.g., the stomach; organs make up systems, e.g., the digestive system). Stem cells are generic template-types of cells the body produces that can be programmed to become specific kinds of cells. And there are even different types of stem cells that the body produces in order to continue to manufacture the new specialized cells in its different tissues. Stem cells are produced in various tissues and organs as their own special replacements and building blocks. The body is constantly renewing most of its tissues with new cells. An individual's genes, inherited from his or her parents, determine all the variations within the individual. New cells are formed when the DNA within an individual cell duplicates, and the cell subsequently divides into two identical cells. However, sometimes things happen in the duplication process, and there are mutations that occur, and thus a variation in a new cell occurs, a mutation that is permanently encoded in its DNA. When that new cell with the mutated DNA then divides, even more mutations can happen.

The cells of the body must communicate with each other to work together. They do this through the incredible design of their cell walls. Mutations can cause communication problems within the new cells. One such problem is a hypersensitivity to growth signals from the organism. These new mutated cells magnify the messages that are sent to signal their time to grow, and they begin to divide at a much higher rate than the normal cells of the surrounding tissue. These cells that are multiplying too rapidly can segregate and become a tumor, continuing to reproduce themselves at a much too high rate, to the detriment of the tissue and organ. Eventually, they crowd out the good cells that are doing the work essential to proper functioning.

Thus, a tissue breaks down, an organ begins to malfunction or not function at all, and a systemic failure is in the offing. Cancer cells can be said to "make it about themselves," both sending and receiving information incorrectly—wrong information that is damaging to the organism at large. This is what subjectivity does to humanity. People wrongly make it about themselves—rather than the collective human "tissues, organs, and systems" in which they are designed to function. They receive and communicate bad information that at least causes short-term problems, and eventually might prove morally, socially, or spiritually damaging, or even cataclysmic to individuals, groups, and even humanity at large. In the New Testament, James expresses the outcome of spiritual and social subjectivity, saying,

> What causes wars, and what causes fightings among you? Is it not your passions that are at war in your members? You desire and do not have; so you kill. And you covet and cannot obtain; so you fight and wage war. You do not have, because you do not ask. You ask and do not receive, because you ask wrongly, to spend it on your passions.[13]

Self-centeredness, manifesting itself as subjectivity, is the ultimate cause of fights and wars. As humans, we tend to make it all about ourselves, and we end up hurting and even killing each other, one way or another, in order to try obtain what we want. However, God will not grant our prayer requests when we are thinking and behaving in this way, because it is our passions—our deceived hearts alone—that are driving these kinds behaviors.

Lies and false teaching are like cancer cells. Mysteriously, misinformation, deliberate or not—rumors, lies, false teaching—has a way of spreading much more rapidly than truth, and it corrupts the inner workings of the individuals and collective groups that believe it.. On the other hand, objectivity allows each of us to properly evaluate and correctly receive information, and to accurately communicate to those around us the information we receive. This allows us individually and collectively to function more effectively and efficiently in our ongoing social interdependence. Objectivity in individuals serves as an ongoing check to misinformation that is constantly being spread through spiritual and social communities and societies at large.

Prayer: Father, help me to see my temporary, finite self from the perspective of the eternal, infinite truth of you, the Creator and the Lord of all that is. Lead me today on the narrow road to life and away from the broad road to destruction. Help me to choose wisely. Help me to choose the fruit from the Tree of Life.

Teach me to be objective regarding myself and the world. Defeat me in my lapses into subjectivity. Help me to know the truth that sets me, as well as all humanity, free.[14]

Reflection: How might my own subjectivity be negatively affecting my faith and correct view of God? How might my subjectivity be negatively affecting others? How might others' subjectivity be negatively affecting me?

References:
1. "Subjective." Merriam-Webster, 2011. http://www.merriam-webster.com (June 2016).
2. Gen. 2 and 3.
3. "Objective." Merriam-Webster, 2011. http://www.merriam-webster.com (June 2016).
4. Matt. 7:13–14.
5. Ps. 14:1; 53:1.
6. 2 John 7.
7. 2 Thess. 2:3–4.
8. Rom. 1:21–25, 28.
9. Rom. 1:25-32
10. Rom. 3:22.
11. John 14:6.
12. Rom. 10:9-10.
13. James 4:1-3.
14. John 8:32.

4

Yahweh, the Great "I Am"

"I am who I am." That is who God is. That is God's name because it is who God is: Yahweh, Jehovah, the Great I Am. Yahweh is not changing or becoming. He is who he is, who he has always been, and who he will always be. In the Old Testament language, Hebrew, God's name was originally written without vowels as YHWH. Hebrew speakers of the time would have known how to pronounce it.

There was no *j* sound in Hebrew, but some early English translations still transliterated YHWH into English as "Jehovah." Hebrew scholars say the better transliteration is "Yahweh." It is translated as "LORD" (all caps) in many translations today. Amazingly, YHWH is said to have been used over four thousand times in the Old Testament. History records,

> Many of the rules for copying the scriptures dealt with the character and heart of the scribe himself. A scribe had to speak and sing aloud each word as he wrote it. They washed their hands before each writing session, not just to make them clean, but rather to prepare the heart and mind for performing the holy act of writing the Word of God. They also prayed before each session. Writing a Torah is a "mitzvah," a holy act. Before writing "Jehovah," the name of God, the scribe had to clean the pen and wash their entire bodies in a "mikveh," a pool of

natural running water. In writing the scriptures, scribes were careful to show great reverence and respect, even centuries before the Hebrew scriptures were canonized, showing that from the earliest times, these writing were recognized as God's Word.[1]

Those who passed down the sacred scriptures were most careful, reverential in fact, in repeatedly copying the Old Testament manuscripts prior to the invention of better paper and the printing press. They were even more reverential in copying the name of God.

We first learn of God's name identity when Moses, whom God appoints to lead Israel from Egyptian bondage, asks the Lord who he is to tell the Israelites God is—what his name is. God says, "I am who I am. This is what you are to say to the Israelites: 'I am has sent me to you.'"[2] A curious name? Perhaps to us. Is it really a name as we think of names? Not really. The reality is God is who he is. There's no need for a name and another identity. Each of us, as a man or a woman, is called by a name. In most cultures, our given names have no real connection to our identities other than that our parents liked the name or we were named after someone else. Thus, our names usually have little to do with who we are. But God is neither a man nor a woman, although together we are made in his image. God's name *is* who he is, and who God is, in fact, *is* his name.

Who among us can say that? Simply, "I am"? We, in this life, are changing, growing, doing. In this world, in this age, we are all in a doing-and-becoming mode. But God just "is"! The implications of God as Yahweh are fundamental and absolute.

One, he is the fundamental universal truth. God just is, whether anyone likes it or not, whether anyone believes it or not, or whether anyone agrees with him or not. Paul says, "the foolishness of God is wiser than human wisdom, and the weakness of God is stronger than human strength."[3]

Two, he is who he is. God is immutable, unchanging. His character and being are not subject to the life-weathering alterations of time itself. Things change, and God's actions and reactions may vary in different people, times, and circumstances, but he doesn't himself change in his actual being. When we get to know God, we don't have to ever get reacquainted with him again. He doesn't age and he doesn't change. He is the eternal, divine constant.

Three, it means he is eternal, steadfast, and immovable—he's not going anywhere. He is outside of time, and is, himself, unaffected by it because he is its creator.[4] And he is the sustainer of time.[5] It is Christ that shows us the character of God in human form, and thus, it is said of him, "Jesus Christ is the same yesterday and today and forever."[6] People come and go. People change on us, and sometimes in not such good ways. None other is constant but God.

Four, it means he is not contrived by or created by humankind. The psalmist contrasted idols with Yahweh in this way,

> Our God is in heaven; he does whatever pleases him. But their idols are silver and gold, made by human hands. They have mouths but cannot speak, eyes but cannot see. They have ears but cannot hear, noses but cannot smell. They have hands but cannot feel, feet but cannot walk, nor can they utter a sound with their throats. Those who make them will be like them, and so will all who trust in them.[7]

There is great comfort in knowing that God is not generated by humanity, but that he generates humanity. He is above the world, and he is in control of it. He can be trusted because no other can supersede him. His word is final. His will is final because he is final!

Five, it means he is different from us. The prophet Isaiah notes that humankind is temporal, and thus, he writes, "The grass withers and the flowers fall, but the word of our God endures forever."[8] Each of us knows our inherent limitations. Therefore, when we must trust other humans like us, we know their inherent limitations. We know we can only, to a limited extent, rely on and trust in others, as their powers and abilities, as ours, are extremely limited in regard to our universe. But God is different, and we can indeed trust him as supreme over all of it.

Six, it means he is independent of humankind, including me! Human power brokers cannot monopolize God. God cannot be manipulated by the crafty. God cannot be politicized by the powerful. He cannot be bought. We don't have to wonder about him. James admonishes believers and says, concerning God, "Don't be deceived, my dear brothers and sisters. Every good and perfect gift is from above, coming down from the Father of the heavenly lights, who does not change like shifting shadows."[9] Each of us can relate to him directly, consistently, and independent of all others. Each believer has the right to become his child, adopted into his kingdom—his eternal household.[10] Good news!

Seven, it means we can trust and depend on him. God is completely reliable because he is who he is and no one can interfere with his decisions, his will, and his work. Humankind can plan whatever we want, but God's purpose will always prevail.[11] No one in all the universe, Satan included, can separate us from God's love.[12]

Yahweh, the Great I Am, through an act of his own grace, has called, and then chosen, each believer. And he has sent us on a mission all our own, collectively and individually. We can set out on this mission in confidence because of the sovereignty of God, given to Christ in this world.[13] And as well because of his love and grace expressed to those who believe in him through Christ.[14]

Inspiration: Epistemology and ontology are two branches of philosophy that study knowledge and existence respectively. Epistemology asks the question: What do we know and how do we know we know it? Ontology asks the question: What actually exists and how do we know it exists? To many, these seem useless, boring, and even nonsensical, but in reality, they force us to think deeply about things important to humanity. Seventeenth-century French philosopher René Descartes contended, concerning how we know we exist, "I think, therefore, I am." Although many have tried to give better explanations for how we know we exist, they all seem a bit, well, odd at best. Human philosophy can, at times, seem painfully theoretical, ambiguous, and speculative, and it can ultimately create more doubt and skepticism than anything else. Living fulfilling and effective lives requires practicality and, yes, faith. We all have to live by faith. We cannot know everything, and as philosophy demonstrates, we don't even agree on what can actually be known in the first place. Thus, the Bible tells us early on, in God's own words using a simple, declarative expression that he just is. He is the basis and template of all existence, and he is the fundamental truth and the foundation of knowledge. Descartes's assertion, "I think, therefore, I am," might also be thought of in this way: "I doubt; therefore, I think. I think; therefore, I am." In other words, one could not doubt without thinking. One cannot think without being. God told Moses to tell Israel, concerning who God is, "I am who I am." The assertion of scripture might thus be summarized as, "There is a creation, and therefore, there is a creator." The reality that humanity would even question—to believe or to doubt—that there is a creator, God, behind our world is perhaps the greatest testimony that God exists.

Prayer: Yahweh, Father, I yield my stubborn, shifting will to you this day in faith and in love. As you have bound up eternity in my heart, please also bind up the reality of your presence within me. Help me to be ever aware of you. Help me to live in you and rely on you. Renew me and conform me to your own image.

Reflection: Imagine what our existence will be like in the next age, when we become as God is, and simply are—just exist in utter contentment—rather than as we are now, living in striving, doing, and becoming? Said another way: What will existence be like without change and the passage of time? What impact should that have upon us in our day-to-day lives?

References:
1. David Raney, "The History of the Bible," Copyright © 1998-2002, (Taken from the Ancient Page, 1998, http://www.biblemuseum.net/virtual/history/ancient2.htm).

2. Exod. 3:14.
3. 1 Cor. 1:25.
4. Col. 1:16–17.
5. Heb. 1:3.
6. Heb. 13:8.
7. Ps. 115:3–8.
8. Isa. 40:7–8.
9. James 1:16–17.
10. John 1:12–13.
11. Prov. 19:21.
12. Rom. 8:38–39.
13. Matt. 28:18–20.
14. Eph. 2:8–10.

5

To Behold Nature Is to Behold God

The objective study of creation is, as many have realized, a study of theology, rather than just a study of the physical and biological sciences. Through these sciences we, in fact, study the invisible God. Through the temporal, we see the eternal. Through the finite, we see the infinite. It is through what we can see that we learn about what we cannot see; we learn about the nature and power of divinity. As we see the artist through his artwork, we see the creator through the creation. The greatest art is, at its core, an expression of the heart of the artist, its creator.

It is the same, as has already been noted, with God. We learn about him, the all-powerful artist, through what he has created. The apostle Paul said, "What may be known about God is plain to them [us], because God has made it plain to them [us]."[1] God has made himself—his existence and his nature—plain.

Our here-and-now reality is that whatever we believe about creation and the origins of the universe; it will ultimately seem unbelievable, out of this world. To believe in a divine creator who could create the universe as we behold it is, admittedly, humanly unbelievable. Where did the creator come from? In a world of cause and effect, as theists, we come to a dead end—"in the beginning, God..."[2] What, or who, then "caused" this creator God? Scripture says he has simply always been. He is eternal and infinite. He is described variously as omniscient (all knowing), omnipotent (all powerful), and omnipresent (present every-where). Wow!

In its best efforts, science has similarly traced the object of its study—creation—back to a big bang, when all matter "exploded" on the scene. Apparently, energy became matter. Science thus comes to its own dead end—E = mc². In plain English, *E*, or energy (measured in joules, J) equals *m*, or mass (in kilograms, kg) times c, the speed of light squared (measured in meters per second). This small but very complex mathematical expression implies many things, one being that energy can be converted to matter and vice versa. It is called the mass-energy equivalence. It implies that small amounts of matter contain very large amounts of energy.

The rise of the theory of relativity began when this belief came about that energy could convert to matter and matter could convert to energy. But in the subsequently proposed big bang theory, where did the energy derive that became the material of this universe? In science, the code word for faith is "theory." A theory is what is believed, not what has been or can literally be proven. A "hypothesis" is a theory that is believed with less certainty and is usually being studied to see if it can be "proven" and become a full-blown theory. As with all human beliefs, if enough people, or the right people, believe them, then they become the conventions of choice. Most, unwittingly, fully accept these theories due to whatever are the present-day, conventional educational, social, scientific, and religious forces of thought and belief.

The reality is that in the end, to believe anything at all, one has to make a judgment call as to their own personal theory, or belief, about origins. And not believing anything is a faith choice all its own. This usually is because we are not willing, or do not feel able, to make a decision. Ultimately, however, we all must live by faith in something or someone. Yes, scientists live by faith just like everyone else, although many scholars seemingly would have us to believe otherwise. And when humans feel they are to be unquestioned, they set themselves up as "gods." When we see them as such, we accept them as gods. Unfortunately, it seems that among humans, we often accept without question the ideas of those who have the right titles or enough notoriety or influence. Thus, we walk by faith in them—these people—and not so much by faith in the beliefs themselves.

Why does it matter? Well, if one is going down a generally pleasant life path but doesn't know where the path leads, one might be wise to pause and ask, "Where are we going?" The path could lead off a cliff; it could lead to a mass execution or annihilation; it could lead to a massive, body-crushing stampede; or it might simply dead-end. Conversely, it could lead to a wonderful paradise. But shouldn't we want to at least try to have a good idea where we are going? And if preparedness is essential for survival, if we can't "know," don't we want to at least speculate and try to move with forethought and purpose? Many have certainly been led blindly down various life paths to all sorts of pain and destruction. The leaders on these destructive paths are usually those most respected and least suspected. The easy paths these blindly-accepted authoritative ones often offer us, ironically, lead at least to disappointment and at worst to tragic consequences.

In a lament of his own, God said to a stubborn, rebellious Israel, before their final defeat and captivity by Babylon,

> I am the Lord your God, who teaches you what is best for you, who directs you in the way you should go. If only you had paid attention to my commands, your peace would have been like a river, your well-being like the waves of the sea. Your descendants would have been like the sand, your children like its numberless grains; their name would never be blotted out nor destroyed from before me.[3]

Israel's choosing to disregard God did not turn out well for them at all. Neither, however, does just any old belief in the divine indicate a positive outcome. In fact, as has clearly been witnessed throughout history, certain misbeliefs about God and their subsequent ideologies have caused even worse outcomes than mere unbelief ever could! Yet the truth is the truth, and it is pure, unadulterated truth that the honest person must seek.

There is a branch of biology called computational biology. Some in this field have set out to compute the odds, in the development of our world, of various of the essential reactions, mutations, occurrences, and such happening by pure random chance. Although these calculations are much debated within science, the odds against all of these events occurring, which are essential to life emerging without divine intervention of some kind, are laughably impossible to most of us! However, that is what those who deny divinity must presently accept. The odds of this universe having self-generated itself into its present form are similar to the odds of winning a lottery millions of times in a row! The former is to be considered no more plausible than the latter, no matter what anyone of any educational, social, or political stature might have us believe.

Countless numbers of people have sat and beheld nature in its wonders, its cycles, its mysteries, and its beauty, pondering its nature and origin. Most still conclude that it all originates from the divine in one way or another. Their wisdom is spoken in the Bible in this way:

> But ask the animals, and they will teach you; or the birds in the sky, and they will tell you; or speak to the earth, and it will teach you; or let the fish in the sea inform you. Which of all these does not know that the hand of the Lord has done this? In his hand is the life of every creature and the breath of all mankind.[4]

Yes, indeed, to study the universe is to study practial theology. It is to study God himself, as he engages and works in his creation.

Inspiration: From the earliest records of humanity, be it in scripture or the findings of anthropology and archeology, it is clear that humankind has believed in the divine. Much of this belief is rooted in an understanding of nature, even to the extent that humans have often ended up worshiping nature itself as God or as the gods. The Bible begins simply, "In the beginning, God created the heavens and the earth."[5] The book of Genesis describes, in sweeping, poetic fashion, the emergence of the creation up until our own time, the age of man. We are presently in the sixth day of creation, so to speak, waiting on the seventh and final day, the after-this-life for us all. For most conscionable people, the atheistic and humanistic explanations for the universe and, even more specifically, for life here on earth, when their roots and ramifications are clearly presented in laypersons' language, seem woefully impossible to most. Only a consideration of the protein molecule alone presents impossible challenges for any spontaneous generation of life. It is said there may be a million proteins in the human body alone. Each one is its own miracle. To make each of the various kinds of proteins requires a specific arrangement of amino acids, said to be the building blocks of life. To make a single type of protein, up to a thousand or more amino acids must assemble in a specific order, or else nothing happens. The odds against that happening are off the charts. No human would ever take such odds in a bet. Its chances of happening merely once would be even less likely than winning a lottery a thousand times in a row! However, humanists suggest that not only did it happen once, but it happened countless times over the eons. The reality is that life is a miracle. Life is supranatural, or beyond what is natural. Each of our existence is a testimony to creation. Our breath is itself a testimony to the reality of creation and the life God breathed into us. Each seemingly miraculous process in our body right now is testimony to a creator. And, especially are our minds, our hearts, and our souls testimonies that the physical emerges from the divine. Not the other way around.

Prayer: Lord, help me seek the pure, unadulterated truth. Help me be brave in seeking the truth and not relinquishing it due to the fear of its life implications, the intellectual intimidation of academia, or because of my own personal desires. Guide me this day to be honest and sincere, a person of integrity. Help me find simple paths to truth amid the complexities and difficulties of understanding both revelation and science. Help me be strong enough to choose which faith I will subscribe to and thus live by, and to accept the responsibility for the outcomes of those beliefs and practices.

Reflection: How might I presently be less than eager about seeking pure, unadulterated truth, when it might conflict with my present beliefs or cause consternation in those around me? Where might that lead me? What or who might most negatively affect my objectivity and openness? What attitudinal changes might be warranted in order for me to be an honest seeker of pure truth?

References:
1. Rom. 1:19.
2. Gen. 1:1.
3. Isa. 48:17–19.
4. Job 12:7–10.
5. Gen. 1:1.

6

The Whole Creation Sings the Song of God

The heavens declare the glory of God; the skies proclaim the work of his hands. Day after day, they pour forth speech; night after night, they reveal knowledge. They have no speech; they use no words; no sound is heard from them. Yet their voice goes out into all the earth, their words to the ends of the world.[1]

Humans have long perceived God through the heavens above us—the vast, endless, amazing universe that sparkles in the night sky. The psalmist declares that the skies proclaim the work of God's hands. Paul says it is through the creation that we can behold God's eternal power and divine nature. Certainly many conclude that the skies demonstrate, through their vastness, their beauty, and their endless complexities, God's incredible power and the universe's divine origin. Unbelievers, however, conclude the opposite.

Countless poems and songs have been written extolling the wonders of the heavens. Gazing into the heavens causes human minds to pursue its secrets and causes, stretching minds, and turning hearts to dreams and even to romance. It causes some to sense their eternal importance, while still others to feel entirely insignificant.

The psalmist, however, tells us that the heavens declare God. Creation sings his quiet song. Isaiah said the purpose of God's word was to make creation a song for those who receive it by faith. He said it would make the world and its landscape sing to us and even applaud us, saying, "the mountains and hills will burst into song before you."[2] The prophet Zephaniah said that God would sing over his people Israel.[3] Music is the language of the heart. Heaven is often depicted as a place of endless song. The lyrics of creation praise its creator.

> Praise the Lord from the heavens, praise him in the heights above. Praise him, all his angels; praise him, all his heavenly hosts. Praise him, sun and moon; praise him, all you shining stars. Praise him, you highest heavens and you waters above the skies. Let them praise the name of the Lord, for he commanded, and they were created. He set them in place forever and ever; he gave a decree that will never pass away.[4]

Again, the psalmist declares that all creation rejoices and sings for God,

> Let the heavens rejoice; let the earth be glad; let the sea resound and all that is in it. Let the fields be jubilant and everything in them; let all the trees of the forest sing for joy. Let all creation rejoice before the Lord, for he comes, he comes to judge the earth.[5]

But the song of creation is not heard with the ears—it is heard first with the mind, and then it is internalized into an experience of the heart. Music feeds the soul and spirit of humanity. The mind knows there is no explanation for creation except for the divine. The mind perceives that before and beyond the physical reality are unseen other dimensions—namely what to us are the "spiritual" ones. It is with the mind that humankind hears the message of creation—all praise be to its creator, God!

The mind perceives it all, but it is with the heart that creation's song is comprehended and experienced. And it is in the heart that human faith, which begins in the mind, finds its own expression. For faith is a straining of the heart, reaching out to the unseen, driven by the conviction of the mind about what is there. "So we fix our eyes not on what is seen, but on what is unseen, since what is seen is temporary, but what is unseen is eternal."[6] The apostle Paul prays for the Ephesian believers that the eyes of their hearts would be enlightened, and similarly, this should be the personal prayer of each of us.[7] We must strain within our hearts to be enlightened regarding what our minds say must exist—a creator, the divine, God. It is foolish to conclude otherwise.

In the concluding book of the Bible, The Revelation, in a grand scene portraying heaven, the elders fall down and worship the God of creation, saying, "You are worthy, our Lord and God, to receive glory and honor and power, for you created all things, and by your will, they were created and have their being."[8]

We too will one day be led in worship in the song all creation sings—the Song of Moses and the Lamb Jesus:

Great and marvelous are your deeds, Lord God Almighty. Just and true are your ways, King of the nations. Who will not fear you, Lord, and bring glory to your name? For you alone are holy. All nations will come and worship before you, for your righteous acts have been revealed.[8]

God's music—his divine expression in the universe—is meant to flow from his heart into each of our heart. He rejoices over us with singing.

Inspiration: Sound is one of the most amazing things. Sound in the form of music is miraculous. Sound is caused simply by vibration. Vibrations send energy in the form of sound waves through air or matter. It becomes sound because of life-forms' ability to pick sound up with eardrums or other means and then to translate it into responsive instincts, thoughts, or perceptions. Sound is everywhere. Vibration itself begins at the atomic and molecular levels. The universe around us is mostly space occupied by minute particles—atoms—assembled into the countless amazing varieties of objects and forms that exist in the universe, from the sun itself, which comprises 99 percent of the mass of our own solar system, to the tiniest bacteria. And all matter vibrates. Each vibration creates a sound wave, however, loud or soft it may be, whether a sonic boom or the faint plop of a water droplet. A sound wave exists independently of being heard or detected by anything in the physical world. The beautiful harmonies we hear are the convergence of two or more sound waves into what is called "constructive interference" patterns (as opposed to destructive interference patterns). Since all matter vibrates, and vibration creates sound, the universe is one unbelievably enormous symphony harmonizing in the song of creation—the song of God. In addition, creation can also be said to dance in beautiful in-step dances, both amazingly complex and marvelously simple. From the song and dance of the atom, with its array of particles—protons, neutrons, electrons, quarks, leptons, and bosons—to the mind-blowing interactions of the galaxies themselves, all are vibrating, thus making sound (at least where there's enough air or matter to carry sound waves), and all are moving in synchronization, thus dancing in a way. The ballroom is the unending universe, the symphony is all the matter, from the largest to the smallest, vibrating within it, and the dance is the interplay of every system in the universe, both the massive and the minute. Thus it can be said that the creation dances and sings the song of God!

Prayer: Father, may my heart sing with all creation the song of the praise of you, its Creator God. May my mind perceive you in all you have made, and may my heart reach out to you in faith. May your living water that has been poured out on all humankind quench the thirst of my soul and my spirit. May the song of my own life be in harmony with the symphony of creation and all your people in singing your praise.

Reflection: Do I hear God through the sounds and sights of the universe? Is my own song in harmony with that of God and his people? If an inside observer were to put words to the song they hear coming from me, what might the name of that song be?

References:
1. Ps. 19:1–4.
2. Isa. 55:12.
3. Zeph. 3:17.
4. Ps. 148:1–6.
5. Ps. 96:11–13.
6. 2 Cor. 4:18.
7. Eph. 1:18.
8. Rev. 15:3–4.

7

Who Are You, Lord?

This is the kind of question that we should all be compelled to ask regularly. The ultimate question might be, "Are you there, Lord?" As seen in the first part of chapter 4, God's clear answer concerning his identity came first to Moses, with God declaring his own name as, "I Am." The next question must then be, "Who are you, Lord?" Not, "Who do I want him to be?" or, "Who do I think he should be?" or, "What do I think he should be like?" Simply, "Who are you, Lord?" It's the only honest way. It's the only question that simply and sincerely seeks the truth.

Saul of Tarsus, a very religious Jewish man who became a follower of Christ and was appointed as the apostle Paul, asked it. He asked it when Jesus appeared to him on Saul's journey to Damascus to persecute Christians. In this incredible story, told by Luke as recorded in Acts 9 and then expounded on by Paul in his own letters, this influential Jewish persecutor of Christians became arguably the most influential Christian leader in history other than Jesus himself! Jesus spoke to him, saying, "Saul, Saul, why do you persecute me?" Luke continues narrating, "'Who are you, Lord?' Saul asked. 'I am Jesus, whom you are persecuting,' he replied. 'Now get up and go into the city, and you will be told what you must do.'"[1]

Saul asked the right question, which got him the right answer, which put him on the right life path. Similarly, it is a wise choice for each of us.

Moses, the leader of Israel in Egypt and on the desert journey, also sought to know God better, asking first who God was and then asking to see him. He said to God, "If you are pleased with me, teach me your ways, so I may know you and continue to find favor with you."[2] God heard and answered the request of Moses. He wants to be with those who want to be with him. God wants to show himself to us—at least to the degree that we can comprehend in this present life, and then fully in the age to come.

To know God, though, one must understand that Yahweh, God, is not a thing. He is not an "it." He is not an idea or a human creation. He has a presence and a personality. God is not to be used and taken advantage of. He's not a mere crutch or contrivance of weak or needy people. He knows us and he knows our hearts. He knows our thoughts, mental and emotional, and he knows the desires behind them.[3] There is no hiding behind duplicity or insincerity in our relationships with him. We can fool others, and we can even fool ourselves, but there is no fooling God!

Yet what we, as fallen humans, are prone to do is to try to control things—especially our relationships, including with the divine. Although perhaps a bit more sophisticated than the ancients, we are still apt to do as they did—create idol gods made in our own image. We attempt to define for ourselves, and for others as well, who God supposedly is based on our own selfish desires and purposes. In our minds, we impose these contrived definitions onto Yahweh and end up with a god wholly different from reality. We end up with a god who is no god at all. We end up worshiping mental and emotional images that exist only in our minds and are in fact "created" in our own image. We simply make these gods up.[4]

Many seem to make God out as a divine insurance policy against eternal destruction. Fire insurance perhaps! They are Christian in order to placate God in this present time, to seemingly insure themselves against the possibility of eternal destruction. Others seem to define God as a divine benefactor or Santa

Claus who will give them not only the things they need, but also the things they want. Others treat him as a divine security blanket to hold near and cuddle during frightening and unsettled times. Still others serve God as their spiritual and emotional badge of honor, which makes them somehow "good." None of these, however, are honorable in any way.

There are all kinds of God definitions to be had. Yet no matter how we might define or see him, God is who God is. "I am who I am."[5] In reality, it matters not who any one of us thinks God should be. Our self-imposed definitions of God do not change the reality of who he is one single bit. And our relationships with these other mental, spiritual, emotional, or otherwise religious idols are meaningless and worse than useless.

In fact, and finally, these made-up fantasy gods only prevent us from finding the reality of the true and living God and experiencing his graciousness and awesomeness. Such gods, in reality, are only a mirror; the "god" looking back at me from the mirror is just me. In this case, the truth is that I am my own god. I define *god* in order to allow or justify whatever it is I want to believe, what I want to be like, or how I want to live. This is most foolish indeed: "They became fools and exchanged the glory of the immortal God for images made to look like a mortal human being [themselves]."[6]

But in reality it is Jesus who "is the radiance of God's glory and the exact representation of his being."[7] Jesus confidently declared that, "Anyone who has seen me has seen the Father."[8] God is real, and Jesus showed us who he really is. We can discover him through creation and the word, and we can experience him through his Spirit, by walking daily with him, and we can be in fellowship with him through his body, the church.

We find him by seeking truth, not seeking what we want to believe, not seeking what we think should be, not seeking out the god that we want. We find the truth of God by seeking out the truth of God, rather than seeking the lie. Jesus said, "The reason I was born and came into the world is to testify to the truth. Everyone on the side of truth listens to me."[9]

Everyone who stands for truth listens to truth. Truth seekers want to know what the truth is, no matter the cost. Proverbs says, "Buy the truth and do not sell it—wisdom, instruction and insight as well."[10] But in this world, we can only approximate the truth based on faith. Faith is what we believe to be true. Certainty is only an expression of a strongly held belief. But the reality is that all that we claim to know is simply what we strongly believe to be the truth.

When the truth is found and believed, it produces hope and conviction. Through such faith, honest and sincere people adjust their reality to it and alter their lives accordingly.

As previously cited at the start of this chapter, in the case of the conversion of the apostle Paul, Luke records this exchange between Saul (who became the apostle Paul) and Jesus, "Who are you, Lord?" Saul asked. "I am Jesus, whom you are persecuting," he [Jesus] replied. "Now get up and go into the city, and you will be told what you must do."[11]

When you find truth, you will find Jesus. When you find Jesus, you will find God. When you find God, you must listen to him, really listen, and he will tell you what you must do. You may not have multiple chances. "Seek the LORD while he may be found, call upon him while he is near."[12]

Inspiration: Humans are self-centered. For something to be alive, in our own self-centered minds, it must be like us. For something to be human, it has to meet some standard determined by us. Ultimately, this is what humanism has always been about. Thus when we look for life, we look for things like us. Many of our standards are arbitrary and set by opinions. We believe reality and truth to be what we conceive and perceive. Thus, to us, hearing is what is done with our ears. Anything we cannot hear is not real. Still, we know in actuality that is not the case, but we persist in acting like it anyway. Since sound is caused by vibrations, which send energy through air and matter in the form of sound waves, and since there are frequencies and levels, which a typical human eardrum cannot pick up, we must admit there are many sounds that exist that we simply cannot perceive. There are also many organisms that do not have eardrums as such but which can pick up and respond to sound waves. Snakes, for instance, do not have ears like ours, but they do have inner ear-type structures to pick up vibrations from the air through their jaws. They also have sensory perception in their skin to pick up vibrations from the ground. But, ultimately, what we call sound is but a perception of the brain, which is related, interpreted, and thus experienced, be it pleasantly or unpleasantly. Also, the human ear can hear many sounds at once, and the brain is capable of focusing in on only one or two at a time while ignoring others. People that live near train tracks, factories, or other loud areas often develop the ability to ignore the constant and otherwise obvious noises. Since sound is perception, can we thus "hear" things in ways other than through eardrums? There are many waves in our universe that travel to us and even through us. What if we actually have the ability to perceive them but have just developed the ability over eons to ignore them or have even lost the ability to perceive them? What if there are other types of communication that we have the ability to perceive but that we haven't learned to detect and interpret? In reality, this is the way it is with God. The divine communicates to us in ways that we must learn to perceive and interpret just as children must learn to hear and interpret language. Perhaps, the new humanity, presently being recreated in Christ, is only regaining spiritual perception abilities that were lost in the Fall.

For instance, for many of us the sound of the birds is just that—the sound of the birds. But to those who have studied and learned to appreciate all the different sounds birds use, hearing birds is highly meaningful, informative, and beautiful. Many of us believe it is that way with "hearing" the divine. Such individuals believe they have developed their capabilities to hear God. Asking how they can know it is God speaking is like asking any of us how we know we are hearing anything. It's a fair question because delusions and dreams demonstrate that we can think we hear sounds that do not exist. But still, each of us might be wise to ask ourselves if we have the capabilities to perceive communication that does not come via our eardrums, but through our minds, our hearts, or our souls—our spiritual antennas. Many believe we do. Perhaps we have been hearing from God our whole lives and have just inadvertently tuned it out as unimportant noise. Just perhaps, no, most assuredly, we have all missed out, at least to some extent, on hearing God as we are truly capable of!

Prayer: Father, help me to ask the right question, as did the apostle Paul, "Who are you, Lord?" Help me to hear and perceive the answer aright, so I can come to hear better the truth and wisdom that flows from you. Help me to perceive and sense your existence and your presence. May I hear you, and may I see you. And help me not to just be a hearer of your voice, but help me be completely responsive to your word and your will.

Reflection: Have I sought to truly hear God? Do I discount important spiritual thoughts as only a mental activity of my own brain? Does my faith in God extend to believing that he can work in me? Do I strive to walk by faith in God in everything?

References:
1. Acts 9:4–6.
2. Exod. 33:13.
3. 1 Chron. 28:9.
4. Rom. 1:21–25.
5. Exod. 3:14.
6. Rom. 1:22–23.
7. Heb. 1:3.
8. John 14:9.
9. John 18:37.
10. Prov. 23:23.
11. Acts 9:5-6.
12. Isa. 55:6.

8

Humanity Bears the Image of Its Creator

"So God created mankind in his own image, in the image of God he created them; male and female he created them."[1] "Then the Lord God formed a man from the dust of the ground and breathed into his nostrils the breath of life, and the man became a living being."[2] We are created in God's image. We have God's DNA. We are alive, as God is alive. And God is all about life; in fact, his whole creation is about life.

But what is life? Is it merely to be defined as the opposite of death? Is it only the presence of breath? Is it determined by the presence of carbon atoms? Is it to be defined as being able to think and reason? Is it feeling? Is it merely the terminus of a big bang and evolutionary processes? Or is life more than breath or reproductive ability or internal systemic processes?

The Bible defines life in terms of God. *Zóé* (Greek) means "life as God experiences it," not just life in the physical and in the present, but life that transcends this present world and age.

Jesus said he was "the life." Jesus doesn't just bring life; he is life.[3] The apostle John writes, "In him was life, and that life was the light of all mankind."[4] Jesus said, "I am the resurrection and the life. The one who believes in me will live, even though they die; and whoever lives by believing in me will never die."[5]

God is about life because he is life. But sin destroys life: "In the day you eat of it [fruit of the forbidden tree] you will die."

Sin corrupts life. Sin deforms life. Sin abuses life. Sin disfigures life. Sin destroys life.

And it is this life that God breathed into humanity—his own kind of life. He gave humankind souls and spirits, as well as living bodies, hearts, and minds. He gave us life, and only he can sustain that life. In fact, he sustains everything.[6] But sin can kill that life: "But you must not eat from the Tree of the Knowledge of Good and Evil, for when you eat from it, you will certainly die."[7]

But Christ is the Tree of Life. He is not only life; he brings freedom to the living: "Now the Lord is the Spirit, and where the Spirit of the Lord is, there is freedom."[8] Eve explained this freedom to the serpent in her own words: "We may [freely] eat fruit from the trees in the garden, but God did say, 'You must not eat fruit from the tree that is in the middle of the garden, and you must not touch it, or you will die.'"[9]

It is this life of God, that we receive from him, that sets us apart from the rest of creation. Each human has a soul, a spirit, a conscience, an awareness, a presence, a personality, a purpose, and a memory. Humans anticipate, feel, retain knowledge, are creative, worship God, and solve complex problems. Humans can experience life as God does because we are made in his image.

But humanity's fall into sin brought a curse on human life: "for dust you are and to dust you will return."[10] And the progression of sin reached its pinnacle in the disfigurement and death of Jesus Christ on the cross—a beating, a crown of thorns pressed into his brow, an agonizing crucifixion, a spear into his heart. It was the prophet Isaiah who foretold what it was to come, saying, "But he was pierced for our transgressions; he was crushed for our iniquities; the punishment that brought us peace was on him, and by his wounds, we are healed."[11]

By his wounds we are healed. He gave us our life at our conception: "For you created my inmost being; you knit me together in my mother's womb."[12] And he offers us a second chance through Christ—eternal life, life as God knows it. "The one who believes in me will live, even though they die; and whoever lives by believing in me will never die."[13] In the world, all will die. Yes, we all have an appointment with the death of our bodies.[14] But in Christ, we find the offer of a resurrection and a life beyond this one.

Jesus himself rose and came back to life in the body that was crucified. Unbelievable? For sure. But true? Yes, ask the apostles who laid their lives on the line vouching for it! "When they heard that Jesus was alive and that she [Mary] had seen him, they did not believe it."[15] But later, they did believe. Jesus said to Thomas, who at first doubted Jesus's resurrection: "Put your finger here; see my hands. Reach out your hand and put it into my side. Stop doubting and believe."[16]

Thus, "He is not the God of the dead, but of the living, for to him all are alive."[17]

He gives us the fallible life of this present age, and in Christ, he gives to each believer the eternal life of the age to come. He heals our deformity and disfigurement once and for all. "By his wounds we are healed."[18]

He saves us and, over time, restores the glory to us that humankind lost at the Fall. He will make all things new for us in his own time. All the corruption, the deformity, the disfigurement, and the death will be removed and will be no more.

> "Death is swallowed up in victory."
> "O death, where is thy victory?
> O death, where is thy sting?"[19]

Inspiration: Genetics is an amazing thing. The power locked in deoxyribonucleic acid (DNA) is seemingly supernatural, reflecting so much about God's divine nature. DNA might be said to be the first level of intelligent matter. There is an account of a gymnast born without any legs and with her heart on the wrong side—a messed-up bit of DNA caused it. Her name is Jen Bricker, and she was given up for adoption when she was born. Her biological mother never even held her before she was taken away at the insistence of her domineering husband. Jen did not know anything about her biological family until she was older. It all turned out well for her though. She would later talk of her adoptive parents and brothers as being "amazing," saying they would never let her use the word "can't," but rather taught her she could do whatever she wanted. She learned how to swim, roller-skate, play volleyball and softball, power tumble, and spin from silk ribbons thirty feet in the air—all without the help of normal legs. Somewhere in the cell division process after the zygote stage, a genetic mishap occurred. Jen grew and developed deformed and physically disabled. As she grew up, she developed an unlikely love of performing gymnastics. She developed her skills all the way to the competition level. After four years of competition, she won a state championship in power tumbling, and in 1998, she placed fourth in power tumbling in the Junior Olympics, the only physically challenged person to compete at such a level. She received the United States Tumbling Association's Inspiration Award. She has continued a career in performance acrobatics.

Growing up, she idolized a young US Olympic champion gymnast named Dominique Moceanu, who, in 1996, charmed the world with her gold-medal-winning performances and beautiful smile. Just a few short years later, Jen would learn this beautiful and extremely talented Olympic gymnastics champion was, in fact, her biological sister! Eventually, they were reunited. To anyone who saw them together, it was easy to see they were sisters. But the point here is that the older developed normally, and developed a love of gymnastics and became an international champion. The other, without a single clue about her biological sister but with similar genetics, developed the same love of gymnastics and was arguably the more amazing of the two gymnast sisters. Although there was a genetic mess up that left her without the use of normal legs, Jen became an outstanding gymnast in spite of the challenges.

It is the same with all of humankind. We have genetics, physical and nonphysical, that we inherit from God. We are made in God's image, and Jesus is our genetically flawless older brother. Although sin (the spiritual genetic mishap) has left us deformed and disabled, just as with Jen Bricker, we all still have within us incredible power and ability inherited from God. And our hero, Jesus Christ, is, in fact, our brother! In spite of our here-and-now "disabilities," we can still have beautiful smiles, and we still resemble Jesus. We are image bearers, although, at present, sin has left us with this spiritually genetic mishap. The deformity caused by sin has caused in humankind the inevitable propensity of each person to sin.[20] But God promises one day that he will remedy all this for those who believe.

Prayer: Father, help me to look in the mirror and be able to see your eternal DNA in my flesh and spirit. Help me to grasp, in the midst of my fallen state and the sin damage I now experience, how truly talented and able I really am. And help me to see how you can do more in me than I can ask or imagine, according to your power that you will place within me if I will only believe.[21] Although sin's deformity appears in my flesh, may your effervescent smile be on my face and may your endless determination be in my heart. Because of my faith in you, may I not use the word "can't" in regard to what I am capable of doing because of your ingenuity and power that works in me.

Reflection: What of the nature of God might I observe even in unbelievers? What of God's nature might I see in my pre-Christian self? What of God's nature might I see since I came to believe? How might the story of Jen Bricker inspire me in my life for God as an image-bearer?

References:
1. Gen. 1:27.
2. Gen. 2:7.
3. John 14:6.
4. John 1:4.
5. John 11:25–26.
6. Heb. 1:3.
7. Gen. 2:17.
8. 2 Cor. 3:17.
9. Gen. 3:2–3.

10. Gen. 3:19.
11. Isa. 53:5.
12. Ps. 139:13.
13. John 11:25–26.
14. Heb. 9:27.
15. Mark 16:11.
16. John 20:27.
17. Luke 20:38.
18. Isa. 53:5
19. 1 Cor. 15:54-55.
20. Rom. 5:12.
21. Eph. 3:20–21.

9

Jesus Christ Demonstrates Perfection in an Imperfect World

Even with all the observable variations among humans of all ages, geneticists have long reported that we are 99.9 percent genetically the same. Although some now debate this, claiming similarity may be as low as 90 percent, depending on what is considered "the same," the point here is that all humans are of the same seed line, the same family. Most of the differences are not necessarily harmful or helpful but only allow for the essential variations among humankind that develop due to mating combinations, adaptations, and genetic alterations. But genetically, we are all, as humans, at least 90 percent and perhaps as much as 99.9 percent the same.

There has also been another variation—a spiritual variation of sorts—that has occurred in all humans, however, and it is most harmful to us all. It is caused by sin. Just as physical forces cause DNA mishaps to occur—mutations—that often leave permanent genetic scars that may be passed down from generation to generation, sin has done the same to the human spirit and soul. It causes us to look, to varying degrees, spiritually disfigured and deformed. As God said to Cain, after Cain had sinned by killing his brother, Abel, "Why is your face downcast?"[1] Sin, in fact, leaves us all "downcast"—handicapped and troubled.

But Jesus came into the world undamaged in soul and spirit. Although he inherited the human genetic scarring from his mother, Mary, Jesus was, in soul and spirit, unmarred by sin.[2, 3] And he showed us the glory of God, our "genetic" Father.[4] He displayed before us the exact human representation of God's being—his personality and his presence.[5] He demonstrated to us that we are made "fearfully and wonderfully."[6]

And Jesus's mission is to repair the damage that the curse of sin has wrought on humankind and to renew us into God's image again. He said, "I am making everything new!"[7] In fact, he is recreating humanity.[8] Through him, we are able, even in our imperfect state, to imitate God as dearly loved children, rather than fear him as insecure slaves.[9] In Christ, God determined from creation to see his chosen ones as "holy and blameless."[10]

But sin is to humanity what rust is to iron. It is not something new; it is the corroding of what is here. Sin is not the opposite of right; it is the corruption of it. Evil is not the opposite of good; it is the decay of good. Sin finds its definition and existence not within itself; sin finds its very existence in all that is, by definition, good. Good can exist without sin; sin cannot exist without good. And only God is good.

This world was made by God and for God.[11] All the processes that exist both spiritually and physically—if these two can, in actuality, be considered as truly separate—were themselves made for God's purposes. There are no accidents. God is sovereign in his created world, his holy temple. Jesus is Lord.[12] Thus, it all turns out as he planned it to turn out. And no forces can resist him for long. No forces have any chance of defeating him at all![13] The present sin and darkness will prove only temporary and will serve God's ultimate redemptive purposes.

Jesus is, indeed, what "done-right-looks-like." He is perfection personified because he shows us God: "No one has ever seen God, but the one and only Son, who is himself God and is in closest relationship with the Father, has made him known."[14] And Jesus has called each of us back to the perfection of God, in whose image we are created: "Be perfect, therefore, as your heavenly Father is perfect."[15] Jesus has called us back to our original form—good. Very good, in fact.[16] He is calling us to the perfection humankind possessed in the beginning and that he promises to fully restore at our final redemption. It is perfection devoid of the corruption that sin causes us. And this perfection is not based on performance but on faith, as it was intended in the Garden of Eden.

In Christ, God frees us from the control and corruption of evil so that he, by his own Spirit, can transform us back into his image.[17] Ours is to simply and determinedly behold him and surrender to his will, allowing his own Spirit to conform us to God's likeness. The outcome is infinitely worth it!

Inspiration: Iron bears the symbol Fe, from the Latin *ferrum*, meaning iron. Its atomic number is twenty-six. It is believed to be the tenth most abundant element in the universe based on mass, making up 34.6 percent of the earth. Almost all life forms require iron to live. Iron is from group VIII on the periodic table—the metals. It is a strong, lustrous, malleable, silver-gray metal. It constitutes 95 percent of all the metal used worldwide. Yet iron is chemically reactive and dissolves readily in dilute acids. Thus, it easily rusts. Rust is formed when water comes in contact with iron. Carbon dioxide in the air combines with water to form a weak acid, carbonic acid. A reaction then occurs with the iron at the surface, forming iron oxide, Fe_2O_3, or rust. Corrosion forms on the iron surface. Since iron is being taken from the surface and turned into iron oxide, the rust literally eats away at the surface, leaving it crusted and marred. Thus, rust only exists because iron exists. It finds its existence only in the life of iron. Sin is that way with humanity. It only exists because of the good that is designed into us. And just as rust is not iron's counterpart but is merely a corruption of it, so it is with evil and good. It is that way because Satan, the champion of all evil spirits, is not God's equal but only his evil counterpart; he is simply a much weaker rival that is doomed by the strongest essential element of the entire universe—God. Sin "rusts" humans just as water and air rust iron. But this rusting can be prevented by the word and Spirit of God being in and on us, just as oil can prevent rusting by preventing water from coming in contact with the iron itself and, even once rust has already formed, by keeping any more air from contacting the iron surface. One day, God will take all the corrupting, corroding influences away. God has already condemned sin itself and, in the end, will finally and permanently take it and its curse away.[18, 19] And finally, the collective "face of believing humanity" will no longer be "downcast."[20]

Prayer: Father, give me the hope—the very real expectation—that you are making all things new and are preparing us all for the day when the corrupting presence of sin will be no more, and we will forever exist in the pure and pristine state you made us, that we will shine as you shine, and that we will no longer experience sin's corrosion.

Reflection: How do you see that sin has corroded, or rusted, the good that is in you or others? What is your role in removing this corrosion and preventing its return? Describe the process of how you have experienced sin's corruption beginning and taking root in your own life? Describe how you may have experienced God arresting this process and beginning to heal you?

References:
1. Gen. 4:6.
2. Heb. 2:17.
3. Heb. 4:15.
4. John 14:9.
5. Heb. 1:3.
6. Ps. 139:13–16.
7. Rev. 21:5.
8. Eph. 2:14–15.
9. Eph. 5:1–2; Rom. 8:15.
10. Eph. 1:4.
11. Col. 1:16.
12. Matt. 28:18.
13. Rom. 8:31–39.
14. John 1:18.
15. Matt. 5:48.

16. Gen. 1:31.
17. 2 Cor. 3:18.
18. Rom. 8:3–4.
19. 1 John 3:5.
20. Rev. 21:3–4.

10

Faith Is the Fundamental Human Assignment

Our assignment is not to try to be what we patently are not, that is, try to be God. Being our own god means we must try to run our lives by knowing good and evil, right and wrong. Rather than attempting to be what we patently are *not*—God, our job is to be what we patently *are*—human. Human is what we are designed to be and qualified for.

It really comes down to the two trees of the Garden of Eden, the two ultimate life choices. They were called the Tree of the Knowledge of Good and Evil, which brings death, and the Tree of Life, which brings life.[1, 2] Satan fooled humankind about the former, the Tree of the Knowledge of Good and Evil, saying, "For God knows that when you eat from it, your eyes will be opened and you will be like God, knowing good and evil." Satan's ruse here, as with most evil deceptions, is a big, ugly lie cloaked in partial truth. In this case, it was the lie of all lies, as it was in fact the eternal human trap.

In the beginning, God gave humankind three assignments: to multiply and fill the earth, to take care of the Garden, and as noted, to not eat of the bad tree.[3, 4] Adam and Eve represent all humanity. The garden represents the whole earth. The trees represent the two ultimate human choices about how to view and act on the world: humanism or theism; a human-centered world or a God-centered world; death or life; temporal or eternal; legalism or faith; human knowledge or trust in God.

But man and woman were soon to be corrupted, and sin would take its deadly toll. Temptation came upon Adam and Eve—humanity—and they made a very bad choice, wrongly and devastatingly thinking they could be as God. Sin deceived them and made them believe a tragic lie. When the wrong choice was made, they realized they were naked, and they were ashamed of it. They hid from God and told him they were hiding from him because they were naked. How ridiculous is that? God asked them, "Who told you that you were naked?"[5]

But still, apart from God, we are all often ashamed. And we all foolishly try to hide from the divine God. It started with the first sin and has continued since.

The reality is that a sinful world often treats us as fairly worthless apart from what we can do for it. It uses and abuses us in the most shameful ways. We are left with faces downcast in all kinds of sadness, shame, depression, despair, helplessness, and hopelessness. We try all sorts of human remedies, both legal and illegal, to relieve our guilt and alleviate our pain—alcohol, drugs, sex, abuse, crime, worldly success, and so forth.

None of it works though, as God infers in his rhetorical question, "Why spend money on what is not bread and your labor on what does not satisfy?"[6] Only God's holy and divine way—his truth—can alleviate the pain of the awful original choice. And only God's way can keep it in remission in a believer. Only God's truth can completely satisfy the inner yearning of a pained and starving spirit.

The best of humankind is capable of awful motives, thoughts, and deeds if left unchecked by the way and will of God. Sin is 100 percent contagious too—all humans catch it. And apart from Christ's healing, it has a 100 percent mortality rate! Because of it, each of must face the death it causes, "For the wages of sin is death, but the gift of God is eternal life in Christ Jesus our Lord."[7] And the damning truth is that, we "all have sinned and fall short of the glory of God."[8]

Who tells us we are "naked"? Who tells us to be ashamed? Who tells us that we are worthless? Who convinces us that we are unlovable and unloved? Who makes us think we must do it all by ourselves; that we are on our own? Who told you that you had to be completely self-reliant and self-contained? Who told you that you wouldn't really die if you were "normal" and went and "sowed your wild oats"?

The original tempter and the accuser of humankind did, that's who!

Yes, everyone must live by faith in God. Even if we could truly say we know anything, we most assuredly can say that no one knows everything. In actuality, it can be argued that all human knowledge is really only a more certain faith in something. It is what we strongly believe to be true. Thus, we all must end up living by faith in something or someone. We must choose to put our chips on either the-here-and-now—the finite, or on eternity—the infinite. We must choose to trust in humankind's knowledge or God's knowledge; our own subjective inner "truth" that we simply contrive or an objective truth and reality outside of and independent from us.

Most sensible people will concur that you cannot completely trust any human or group of humans to know and do all that is right. We are notoriously imperfect. None of us can completely trust even ourselves. Even if self-trust were a viable life option for us, we are incapable of even knowing and comprehending all that is good and evil in the first place. Thus, we even fall into the trap, as ancient Israel did, of calling "good evil and evil good."[9]

Through Christ, God then reintroduces and redefines where life can be found—in a trust relationship with him. Jesus is the ultimate Tree of Life, because he is life itself.[10] Jesus says the very work that God requires of each of us is to believe in him, not ourselves.[11] The apostle Paul says that, in the gospel of Christ, righteousness—being aright with God—is something God gives us or assigns to us, in his own mind and way of seeing things.[12] He sees us as righteous because of our faith that he is righteous. In and through Christ, the requirements of the law—the rules and requirements of good and evil—are completely fulfilled for us if we will live by faith and walk in God's Spirit, through whom Jesus comes to us.[13]

Trust in God—having faith in who he is and what he does for us—is humanity's fundamental assignment. It was the assignment in the beginning, and it is the assignment till the end. A right relationship with God has always been based on him and on our trusting him completely. Adam and Eve messed it up; Jesus Christ fixed it. And true trust—faith—is always manifested in obedient responses and efforts, not to human traditions, teachings, and self-serving interpretations, but to the true will of God for us: transformation back to our real image and nature—his.[14, 15]

Inspiration: Jesus said that all things were possible for those who believe.[16] There are many examples of the great accomplishments of those who simply believed something was possible. Gandhi hoped against hope for an independent India. It was his faith that prompted it. Against seemingly insurmountable odds, Nelson Mandela believed racism and apartheid could be ended in South Africa. Even after serving twenty-seven years in prison for the injustice he suffered at the hands of a white minority government, he ultimately became the first black leader of his country. He then led in the dismantling of institutionalized racism that had long existed there. Martin Luther King Jr. had a dream of equality, not just for blacks in America, but for all people. As a believer and a Christian pastor, he used the same nonviolent approach that Christ taught us and that Gandhi and Mandela also used. King was arguably the greatest contributor to the continuing dismantling of institutionalized racism in America, leading in the passage of the Civil Rights Act in 1964. Trusting and imitating Jesus, Christ's "unschooled, ordinary" apostles spread the gospel message that would found the ever-expanding Kingdom of God on earth.[17] There are many extraordinary examples from the biblical story of those who trusted God and all that they were able to accomplish because of their trust.[18] Paul says that God can do in each of us more than we can ask or imagine because of his power working in us.[19] If we believe, each of us can do the same kinds of things as those great examples from the past. All things truly are possible to those who have faith in Christ!

Prayer: Father, help us to make having faith in—truly trusting in—Jesus the center of our work for you. May we see the evidence and substance for a strong faith in the story and life of Jesus, in all the other compelling stories of scripture, and in the incredible examples of the faithful who have gone before us in more recent history. Stir within us, O Lord, a robust and living faith that keeps us close to you.

Reflection: How is my work of believing in Jesus going, and how can I improve? Who are some examples of people I know who demonstrate the power of faith in our lives?

References:
1. Gen. 3:5.
2. Gen. 3:22.
3. Gen. 1:26–27.
4. Gen. 2:15.
5. Gen. 3:11.
6. Isa. 55:2.
7. Rom. 6:23.
8. Rom. 3:23.
9. Isa. 5:20.
10. John 14:6.
11. John 6:29.
12. Rom. 1:16–17; Eph. 1:4.
13. Rom. 8:3–4.
14. James 2:14–26.
15. Matt. 15:1–9.
16. Mark 9:23.
17. Acts 4:13; 17:6.
18. Heb. 11.
19. Eph. 3:20–21.

11

The Worst Blindness Is the Blindness of the Heart

The apostle Paul wrote in his letter to the Roman church, concerning unbelieving Israel, that "if you declare with your mouth, 'Jesus is Lord,' and believe in your heart that God raised him from the dead, you will be saved. For it is with your heart that you believe and are justified, and it is with your mouth that you profess your faith and are saved."[1] It is one thing to believe something with the mind; that is mental ascent to a thing, and all faith must ultimately originate there. It is completely another to believe something with your heart, because that means internalizing it, giving oneself over to it, and allowing it to drive behavior. Biblical faith is a straining of the heart to grasp and experience the invisible creator God and his Son Jesus Christ.

Blindness of the eyes is a terrible handicap for humans because we are so dependent on our vision for our quality of life and even our survival. We are most inspired by the stories of those who deal bravely with their blindness. But blindness of the heart is even worse, because it is the heart that controls behavior. Our eyes see things and our mind interprets what is detected. The mind records information. The mind thinks and reasons out logically. The mind ultimately can determine what goes into the heart, and, once something is in the heart, it takes root and expresses itself in our identity, and thus, our behavior. God says the human heart is deceitful, and it is our hearts and our minds that he sees and searches out.[2] God sees us as being what are hearts are. Humans look at outward appearances and behaviors because that is what God has given us the ability to do.[3] God, however, can and does look at our hearts because they define us; they tell our whole story.

Christ's teachings and commands are first and principally aimed at the heart and mind—our character. Christ intends for us to *become,* and not just act, "poor in spirit," "meek," "pure in heart," and so forth.[4] In fact, Jesus sums up what it means to obey the whole Law of Moses in terms of, first and foremost, an inner obedience of God within our charcter, saying the overarching and summarizing commandment of the law is to love God with all of our heart, our soul, and our mind, and then to love your neighbor as yourself.[5]

Jesus taught that it is out of the heart that our evil behavior emerges.[6] Proverbs says everything we do flows from it.[7] Jesus said, "A good man brings good things out of the good stored up in his heart, and an evil man brings evil things out of the evil stored up in his heart. For the mouth speaks what the heart is full of."[8] What is in the heart is what comes out in our behavior—it is the fruit by which we can know who a person really is.[9] One's faith can finally be known and thus imitated by considering the outcome of their way of life, the fruit of their lifestyle, because the ultimate outcome of our way of life cannot be faked.[10]

Talk is cheap and can easily be deceptive and even hypocritical. Momentary behaviors can be the same. But the outcome of our way of life—the overall fruit of our life—cannot be hidden for long. God can see the heart; we cannot see the heart, even our own to a great extent. But we can consider the fruit of another's or our own life. It is through the fruit of one's life that the truth about the genuineness of their faith can finally be known.

The mind determines what goes into the heart, but the heart determines what comes out of one's life. Faith is first a mental assessment of and decision about the information, data, and facts available—the evidence and the reasons. True and reasonable faith begins with a decision, be it a conscious or an unconscious one. That decision is then absorbed into the heart for inculcation, incubation, and processing, where it will take root and drive one's behavior.

Although the heart controls behavior, the mind determines what goes into the heart; therefore, the mind is the gatekeeper of the heart. Hence, Paul said we are to be transformed by "renewing our minds."[11] Jesus said that our hearts will be vested most in the things we invest ourselves in the most.[12] That is, what we decide to invest our lives in (our mental decisions) determines what our hearts will actually care about and therefore the kinds of things that we do.

In summary, our true faith is first of the mind and then of the heart. And our lives will tell the reality and story of what our faith is all about. But God knows before the fact because he knows our hearts. The apostle John said, "we know that God is greater than our hearts, and he knows everything."[13] Fortunately, although he knows our hearts, God is greater than our hearts. His grace is sufficient even for the corruption that lies within us, if we will just trust him. Our trust must always be in his goodness and not in our own!

The apostle Paul told the Ephesian church of his prayer for their spiritual growth and development, praying that the "eyes of their hearts may be enlightened."[14] Enlightenment is being able to see something, to finally get it. Our hearts can be hard and dark, the doors tightly shut and locked and the lights turned off. We can be highly intelligent and knowledgeable and still be blind within. And we will miss the invisible—God and his kingdom. In fact, we must be born again to see the kingdom.[15] Concerning the unregenerate of heart, Proverbs tell us, "The way of the wicked is like deep darkness; they do not know what makes them stumble."[16] The apostle Paul wrote, "the god of this age has blinded the minds of unbelievers, so that they cannot see the light of the gospel that displays the glory of Christ, who is the image of God."[17]

Thus, the worst kind of blindness is blindness of a heart that is unenlightened to the reality of the gospel of Christ, because it is the gospel that reveals to us who God really is. And who God really is, is to us, very good news!

Inspiration: Many know the amazing and inspiring story of Helen Keller, who, although she was deaf and blind, broke through the barrier of this kind of physical human darkness like none before her had. With the help of Anne Sullivan, Keller learned to communicate and was the first deaf and blind person to earn a college degree, becoming an author, lecturer, and political activist. However, many have not heard of Laura Bridgman, the daughter of a New England farm family, who, at the age of two, became ill with scarlet fever and subsequently lost her own eyesight, hearing, sense of smell, and most of her sense of taste. Forty years before Keller's achievements began, Bridgman became the first deaf and blind American to learn to communicate enough to achieve a significant level of education.

Most people also know that Anne Sullivan is credited with bringing Helen Keller out of her personal darkness. But what most do not know is that Anne Sullivan had, as a child, suffered a disease that left her nearly blind, and was herself moved to Boston to the Perkins Institute for the Blind. It was there that Sullivan met and befriended a much older Laura Bridgman, a permanent resident at the school. Their friendship is said to have been partly driven by the fact that neither fit in well at the school. It was from Bridgman that Sullivan learned the manual alphabet and most likely gained much of the insight and expertise she would need later to educate Helen Keller. Bridgman and then Keller helped open the eyes of others to the potential of the deaf and blind to be able to, in their own way, "see," "hear," and thus learn and communicate. Although the road was narrow and difficult for each of them, as well as for all those who have followed them, these two dared to overcome their blindness.

Just as malformation and disease deprives many of earthly eyesight, the Bible says that Satan too blinds the spiritual eyes of unbelievers.[17] This includes all of us at some point in our lives, even those who have grown up in the church. Jesus said that the road out of this blindness would be narrow and difficult, but doable and more than worth it. To find God, our minds must learn to communicate with him—to learn his sign language, so to speak—and then our hearts must do the communicating.

Prayer: I ask that you, O Lord, the glorious God and Father of our Lord Jesus Christ, to give me your Spirit, the Spirit of wisdom and revelation, so that I can grow daily to know you better and better. I pray that the eyes of my heart may be opened and enlightened, that all my spiritual blindness be healed and taken away, so that I may truly see the hope—the full and assured expectation—that you have called me to. I pray also that I may see and recognize the tremendous riches of my glorious inheritance as your child and that I may clearly see from within the incomparably great power available to me through my faith in you. Help me to live by the vision of my mind's and my heart's faith, and not first and only by the ability of my mortal eyes and ears. And may my spiritual vision, given to me by you, inspire others to fully see the true light: you, my beautiful and masterful and graceful Lord!

Reflection: Who am I at the heart level? What do I think God sees through his graceful eyes looking within me? Am I doing the difficult in order to be able to see the awesome? How deeply into my heart am I internalizing my faith? Whose faith would I like to influence me the most?

References:
1. Rom. 10:9–10.
2. Jer. 17:9–10.
3. 1 Sam. 16:7.
4. Matt. 5:3–10.
5. Matt. 22:37-39.
6. Matt. 15:19.
7. Prov. 4:23.
8. Luke 6:45.
9. Matt. 7:16.
10. Heb. 13:7.
11. Rom. 12:1–2.

12. Matt. 6:21.

13. 1 John 3:20.

14. Eph. 1:18.

15. John 3:3.

16. Prov. 4:19.

17. 2 Cor. 4:4.

12

Faith Is Not a Feeling; It Is a Decision; It Is Conviction

Most of us associate the heart with feeling. In the Bible, the heart is seen as a part of, or as a function of, the brain, having its own thoughts and, from these thoughts, forming attitudes.[1] Many await some faith feeling in order to believe and embrace God. They rely on their hearts alone to tell them what to believe as well as to guide them through life. "Follow your heart" is their mantra. Faith is seen as a feeling to be expected or sought out, not a reasoning faith of the mind that faces the real challenges of believing beyond what we can see with our mortal eyes. For these, belief in God is an emotional notion to be completely relied upon, be it good or bad. However, to do such is very unwise, because the heart is deceitful and no one can truly understand it.[2] Heart thoughts alone, although powerful and sometimes overwhelming, are often completely unreliable, totally irrational, amazingly illogical, and thus often downright wrong! And it is the exercising of this kind of faith that often inadvertently turns off and turns away many thinking people. This is tragic.

To measure or experience faith merely by one's feelings, emotions, and sentiments, devoid of deep mental, reasoned determinations and conviction, is a grave mistake that is, unfortunately, all too common. It often leads to emotional agnosticism, atheism, or doubt among believers due to hurts, past abuses, unresolved anger, disappointments, loss, personal failures, and so on. Many believe based on their feelings and, conversely, just as many don't believe based on their feelings. Neither of these kinds of faith (or lack thereof) is not so much because of serious, open-minded, objective reasoning, but because of what mostly begins and ends in the heart. Neither of them, in actuality, originates with reason.

Many atheists and agnostics, it seems, don't believe in the divine largely because in their hearts they cannot accept certain perceptions of God or the way the world works. Perhaps because they don't like it, they just deny its existence. The heart is capable of feeling many things—good and bad, happy and sad, trusting and untrusting, and on and on. Just as our ears can hear many sounds, and our noses can smell many scents, so our hearts can feel many things. These responses are natural. The root cause of the problem with a faith that is based primarily on feelings and emotion is with the emotional thoughts themselves. Emotion-based thoughts are untrustworthy, because thoughts coming from emotion are often self-centered, subjective, biased, exaggerated, and so forth, not based on reason and fact but on impulse, conditioning, psychology, and various social factors.

Yet the world would tell us that the heart *is* what we are to follow, as in "follow your heart"! Of course, the deceiver of the world would want to convince us to follow our unregenerate unspiritual hearts. Satan has long known the key to deceiving and blinding humanity is to blind our hearts.

Our hearts are actually often quite deceptive, because they can be badly misguided. The heart can become a stagnant pool of all kinds of ungodly things within any of us. Jesus said it is what comes out of the heart that defiles or corrupts us.[3] And the world has a way of packing our hearts with garbage while robbing them of anything of value! The heart is where evil thoughts and bad attitudes are stored. And the feelings that develop from them can seriously cloud good judgment and lead to evil, because ultimately, it is the heart, not the mind, which most directly produces our behaviors. Thus, uncontrolled hearts can lead us into all sorts of doubt, evil, and foolishness.

We were born into a fallen world with its corrupting cover of sin—think rot, rust, corrosion—eating away at it, both from the inside and the outside.[4] Sin is 100 percent contagious, and its mortality rate is 100 percent as well.[5] However, God, in Christ, raises from the dead those who hear and believe the gospel. God anticipated the human outcome and planned a stunning remedy from the very beginning—Christ's redemptive sacrifice.[6] It is through Christ that God heals the corruption of the human heart and begins removing the corrosion.

In the Bible, true faith is not blind, nor is it based on some inner desire, feeling, or sentiment causing one to *believe* a thing. How many examples does one need to grasp that the heart can be led to believe all sorts of lies? So much of Christian counseling is helping mentally and emotionally troubled individuals stop believing the lies their hearts have believed. So many of us grow up feeling worthless when the truth is we are priceless—at least to the only opinion that matters, God's. We believe we are unwanted when it was God's own breath that breathed life into us in the first place. He clearly wants us, and what opinion is weightier than his? The heart is deceitful, and we need to always remember that, and never thoughtlessly follow it.

True and biblical faith is based on the tangible, the true, and the real (substantive) and is based on evidence (evidential). Genuine faith, as described in scripture, is about confidence and assurance, not merely human fancy and wishes.[7] True faith is, in fact, not a feeling at all. Surely, one will feel their faith, as the heart ultimately follows the mind. But there will just as surely be times when faith will not be felt at all, and often quite the contrary of feeling faith, we might feel significant doubt and unbelief. True faith however defies any of the heart's less-than-desirable present moods and doubts. As we grow in Christ, our conviction grows, and we will indeed feel our faith more and more. We will truly experience the love of God.[8] And we will often feel the peace that passes understanding.[9] Yet still, even the most mature will experience times of fear and doubtful feelings.

Also, the Spirit, when he comes into us through our faith and trust in God, will then bear within us his fruit: "love, joy, peace, forbearance, kindness, goodness, faithfulness, gentleness, and self-control."[10] In this, we will finally be able to sense and feel the Holy Spirit's fruit as it grows and is manifested in us. This is what valid faith feelings are about. These can be trusted because of the rationality and substantiation behind them. However, even after conversion, we will still sometimes feel our fears, doubts, and hurts. A desperate father perhaps expressed these emotions best when he said to Jesus, "I do believe; help me overcome my unbelief!"[11] In actuality, the emotion of doubt is often only just fear and is not based on reality and reasoning. Doubt flowing from fear is frequently based on the basic animal instinct to be safe, to look out for self, and to first and foremost just survive.

We are truly complex beings made in God's image. God gives us the breath of life at birth. As we grow up, at some point, that breath is knocked completely out of us by a gut punch, so to speak, from Satan himself. However, Christ himself breathes the breath of life back into us again. We are raised from the dead. We are regenerated. But we certainly can and will continue to at times feel ambivalence in our faith as well as toward God himself. We must not let these conflicting feelings hinder what we have come to believe in the more reasonable moments of our minds, and we must certainly not let them define what we are to believe moving forward. Entertaining new information, evidence, and revelations that might cause us to doubt our previous decisions is one thing—in fact, honest updating of our faith is right and necessary as we continue to hone our genuine faith—however, giving in to doubt caused by fear is quite another. It is an undesirable option in fact.

The good news is that we are no longer subject to the shifting moods of our fleshly heart. God sees our faith not in our moods of fleshly feeling, but in the core convictions of our reasoning minds, and he sees the decisions we subsequently make in response, especially the ones that defy our fleshly desires. There can, of course, be honest doubts, just as there is honest faith. There too can be doubtful and negative emotions of our hearts, though, that may have little to do with what we have come to strongly believe in.[12] This spirit-versus-flesh, faith-versus-doubt conflict is, of course, remedied only by Christ himself![13]

The pinnacle of faith is not a feeling; it is the deep conviction about what is real and right and the behaviors that follow. The pinnacle that the love of God calls us to stand upon is a conviction about truth and right that rises above mere fleshly desires, sentiments, and emotions. As Jesus asks, "If you love those who love you, what reward will you get? Are not even the tax collectors doing that?"[14] The faith and love to which Christ leads us is reasoned. It is far above the basic human norm. It is lofty and sublime. It is a full mind and heart experience that flows out into confident, purposeful, and meaningful living.

Inspiration: Arguably, dreamers and believers who faced not only their doubts and fears, but also the doubts and fears of others have accomplished all the greatest and most important human feats! At the trial of Christ, Peter at first gave way to his fear, but then just days later, he gave way to his faith. And in doing so, he led the advancement of the kingdom-building gospel into the whole world. Thomas too gave way to his doubt in doubting Christ's resurrection. But after witnessing Christ alive, he faithfully and fearlessly took the gospel into Asia, where he was martyred. Saul of Tarsus doubted Christ and at first fearlessly acted on his doubt in killing Christians. But after seeing and hearing the resurrected Christ, he arguably became the bravest and most faithful of all the disciples.

In a twentieth-century example, Winston Churchill was England's leader in the face of the advancing Nazi army. None had been able to withstand it yet. Many others urged pursuing terms of a peaceful subjugation to Hitler's daunting force. But Churchill's belief in the face of all their doubts was best summarized in a speech he made to students at Harrow School, his alma mater, on October 29, 1941, when England stood alone, at that point in time, in the noble fight against an evil empire.

You cannot tell from appearances how things will go. Sometimes imagination makes things out far worse than they are; yet without imagination, not much can be done. Those people who are imaginative see many more dangers than perhaps exist, certainly many more than will happen, but then, they must also pray to be given that extra courage to carry this far-reaching imagination. But for everyone, surely, what we have gone through in this period—I am addressing myself to the School—surely **from this period of ten months this is the lesson: never give in, never give in, never, never, never, never—in nothing, great or small, large or petty—never give in except to convictions of honor and good sense. Never yield to force; never yield to the apparently overwhelming might of the enemy.** We stood all alone a year ago, and to many countries, it seemed that our account was closed; we were finished. All this tradition of ours—our songs, our school history, this part of the history of this country—were gone and finished and liquidated.[15]

Reasoned faith is not a feeling; it is a conviction; it is a certainty of belief that is based on substance and reason. It is not a feeling, not a sentiment. It is not a desire or a want. It is not generated by the human fleshly nature. It is from above, heavenly. It is a fruit of God's divine Spirit. Such faith overcomes the self-serving mortal feelings of doubt and fear. It exudes the spirit of the likes of Churchill. It exudes the Spirit of Christ. And if we too will pursue such lofty conviction, it will in later years be said of us what was said of our faithful forefathers in earlier biblical times,

And what more shall I say? I do not have time to tell about Gideon, Barak, Samson, and Jephthah, about David and Samuel and the prophets, who through faith conquered kingdoms, administered justice, and gained what was promised; who shut the mouths of lions, quenched the fury of the flames, and escaped the edge of the sword;

whose weakness was turned to strength; and who became powerful in battle and routed foreign armies. Women received back their dead, raised to life again. There were others who were tortured, refusing to be released, so that they might gain an even better resurrection. Some faced jeers and flogging and even chains and imprisonment. They were put to death by stoning; they were sawed in two; they were killed by the sword. They went about in sheepskins and goatskins, destitute, persecuted, and mistreated—the world was not worthy of them. They wandered in deserts and mountains, living in caves and in holes in the ground. These were all commended for their faith, yet none of them received what had been promised, since God had planned something better for us, so that only together with us would they be made perfect.[16]

Truly, the world was not worthy of them because they were not of this present sinful world. And neither should we be.

Prayer: Father, help me not to confuse faith in you with the feelings inside of me. May my faith be reasoned, resolute, substantive, and strong. Help me rise above my momentary feelings and moods that can be mere fleshly instincts and reactions to day-to-day stimuli. Help me, as our forefathers of faith did, to live a life worthy of the gospel, of which the world is not worthy. Help me be in the world, but not of the world.

Reflection: How have I confused my feelings with my faith? How has it negatively impacted my walk with Christ? Why do you think humanity seemingly prefers to live by feelings of the hearts rather than convictions of the mind? What can I do to move forward more powerfully with a biblical faith and conviction?

References:
1. Heb. 4:12.
2. Jer. 17:9.
3. Matt. 15:11.
4. Ps. 51:5.

5. Rom. 3:23; 6:23.
6. Eph. 1:4–10.
7. Heb. 11:1.
8. Eph. 3:17–19.
9. Phil. 4:6–7.
10. Gal. 5:22–23.
11. Mark 9:24.
12. Rom. 7:14–20.
13. Rom. 7:21–25.
14. Matt. 5:45.
15. Winston Churchill, "Never Give In, Never, Never, Never," From a speech at Harrow School in 1941, Source: National Churchill Museum website, https://www.nationalchurchill-museum.org/never-give-in-never-never-never.html.
16. Heb. 11:32–40.

13

Faith Is a Priceless Gem

Anything that does not come from faith in God is sin.[1] That is, God expects us to trust him in all that we do or don't do. The apostle Paul said it. Faith is the foundation of our relationship with God because it is the entirety of our response to God. It is the all-encompassing requirement of any relationship with God. We must trust him in order to know him. In fact, to truly know him is to trust him.

In the Garden of Eden, there were the two special trees. The fruit of the forbidden one, the Tree of the Knowledge of Good and Evil, was to be completely avoided because it is deadly to humanity.[2] Its fruit is still to be avoided because it is just as deadly today as it ever was. The fruit of the knowledge of good and evil is self-reliance. It is humanistic. It is legalistic. It is trusting in self and human ability. And it is not trusting in—having faith in—God. On the other hand, the fruit of the Tree of Life was the truly desirable fruit because it would produce eternal life.[3] All the other trees were surely beautiful, and humanity was free to enjoy the fruit of all of them for their earthly sustenance.[4] Most everything God created was for them to enjoy, but just the one single tree was taboo. And for a very good reason.

For each of us, the world is the garden we live in, full of countless wonderful delights. "We may eat freely from all the trees in the Garden," as Eve said to the tempter. Even the usual day for most of us can be filled with the freedom to enjoy simple, unbelievable, and delectable pleasures. There are so many, and they are so wonderful that we take them for granted. We can come to feel and act as though we are entitled to them, especially if we assume they are merely cosmic accidents that we are just lucky to enjoy. The specters of disability, disadvantage, and death should remind us, however, that we are not.

Even the poorest and most oppressed can behold beauty and wonder all around them, hear music and beautiful sounds, feel incredible sensations, taste delectable flavors, and smell the array of fragrant aromas both nature and human ingenuity produce. The complex interactions of our senses, our minds, our hearts, and our spirits also provide us with many other countless wonderful experiences, such as, loving and being loved in all the many ways available; expressing and enjoying good humor; bearing, loving, blessing, teaching, and enjoying children; producing and enjoying art in all its many expressions; and engaging the spiritual through worship, prayer, and godly service. The list of all we have been given to experience seems endless.

And on top of all of that, we have been given the ability to remember countless wonderful moments that have been given to us. Locked in prison cells and trapped in holes in the grounds, we can allow ourselves to drift into memories of treasured times, or we can travel ahead in anticipation of better times in the future. We are able to take the best of history with us. We can accrue life upon life—that is, if we trust in God, if we have faith.

For faith has the power to turn the bitter into the better. Faith turns hopelessness into hope. The object of our faith—God—gives us valid reason to believe and be optimistic in the ultimate outcomes of it all. Faith turns despair into hope. Faith turns helplessness into strength. Faith turns fear into courage. Faith turns enemies into family and friends. Faith turns hate into love. Faith unifies where there is division. Faith turns problems into solutions. Faith finds cures and healing for diseases. Faith spans oceans; it spans time. Faith is a healing balm for the weary and oppressed. Faith makes all who possess it truly rich and powerful—so rich, in fact, that those who possess it do not need the money and possessions those who lack faith need in order to feel richly blessed. Faith makes us not need those things, for we have found someone and something worth imeasurably more!

Faith cannot be stolen. Faith cannot be destroyed, at least, not without the consent of its owner. Faith cannot be oppressed. Faith cannot be bought; it can't be sold. Faith cannot be conquered, and others cannot control it.

Faith is worth more than gold and precious metals ever could be.[5] Our faith acts as our passports to pricelessness.[6] Faith is the key to life—true, eternal life. We who possess faith are wealthy indeed!

Faith is the gold we are to wear. Faith is the costly gem set in this sparkling gold. And it is the priceless jewel we wear without the shame of greed or gaudiness. "For I am not ashamed of the gospel, because it is the power of God that brings salvation to everyone who believes: first to the Jew, then to the Gentile. For in the gospel, the righteousness of God is revealed—a righteousness that is by faith, from first to last, just as it is written: 'The righteous will live by faith.'"[7] We can wear our faith proudly, confidently, and humbly, without shame or guilt. It does not demean nor does it overly esteem others.

Many who disavow and disregard God see faith as somehow shameful and even silly, choosing foolishly, it is believed by many of us, rather to place their faith in the knowledge claimed by humanity—the knowledge humans possess about good and evil. But such faith is hollow and deceptive.[8] God's foolishness, if there even could be such, would prove much greater than all the human wisdom available.[9] God can always be trusted, and his words will always prove true.[10] It is in believing in and revering the God that is—Yahweh—that the only true wisdom is to be found.[11] Of course, false Gods, the gods human create rather than the God that created humans, are deaf, dumb, blind, and useless. They are but figments of human imagination and control and power mongering.

Faith is our portal to God, is priceless, and is thus worth the effort. Because true faith in Christ is our single, foundational, God-given assignment.[12] It is to be our life work.

Faith indeed is priceless. Nothing is impossible to those who have faith.

Inspiration: Jesus asked his followers two key questions: What good is it for someone to gain the whole world yet forfeit their soul? And, what can anyone give in exchange for their soul?[13] The correct answer to each is: nothing. Our souls—our beings—are the only truly priceless things we possess, for they are the essence of us that can live spiritually and eternally. They are priceless, and they are designed to be eternal. Our souls are the summary of our personhoods, and our very personalities emanate from them. They are our identity. They define us. They are our core. They are our connections to our spirits and all that is spiritual. They are designed to live life as God experiences life—truly and eternally. Yet the fruit of the Tree of the Knowledge of Good and Evil exposes us as sinners and kills us: "For sin, seizing the opportunity afforded by the commandment, deceived me, and through the commandment put me to death."[14] God made it clear that sin was toxic and deadly to every one of us. Its cancerous effects are malignant, contagious, and always fatal to all humanity. Yet God has made a 100 percent effective cure available to all who seek it. Although the penalty for sin—every single sin—is death, God's free gift to us in Christ is life eternal.[15] Faith is a priceless gem because it is our access to what alone is priceless—eternal life with God. And to those who would seek God, faith can make them the richest among all humans, and it is completely free!

Prayer: I believe in you, O God. Christ Jesus, my Lord. I come to you in trust, in adoration, and in surrender, seeking with all my heart your forgiveness, your presence in my life, and your blessing. Be my guide and my refuge. Be my portion and my treasure. Be my purpose and my end. Make your glorious light shine upon me, within me, and from me. And give me peace that passes understanding. May the glorious riches of your grace be made manifest this day in my faithful acceptance of the riches of your blessings and kindness to me. Multiply the blessings given to me to bless those around me.

Reflection: How have I valued my faith greatly? And how have I devalued my faith by accident or on purpose? How might I be able to grow more in my faith?

References:
1. Rom. 14:23.
2. Gen. 2:17.
3. Gen. 3:22.
4. Gen. 2:16; 3:2.
5. 1 Pet. 1:7.
6. Rom. 5:6–8.
7. Rom. 1:16–17.
8. Col. 2:8.
9. 1 Cor. 1:25.
10. Prov. 30:5–6.
11. Prov. 9:10; 1:7.
12. John 6:29.
13. Mark 8:36–37.
14. Rom. 7:11.
15. Rom. 6:23.

14

The Three Facets of Faith

Faith is as a precious gem, even more precious than gold. When seen as it is, it is indeed beautiful. It is our present partial owner-ship of the field with the hidden treasure and the pearl of great price.[1] It ensures us of the riches of our inheritance in Christ.[2]

Faith, however, must not be seen narrowly as a single-fac-eted, one-time event. It must not merely be seen as an ascent to something I accept to be true or wish to have a part in. Faith is not to be a shallow thing. Faith is not to be cheapened on the altar of church growth. Faith is not a quick elixir to a life of fear, doubt, and willful living. Faith indeed starts with a mere glint of thought—a "perhaps." But it ends in an utter conviction and life determination—a "for sure."

I can believe that my wife is my wife and yet still have no faith in her or still be completely unfaithful to her. I can certainly believe my mate is faithful and be unfaithful myself. But God is always faithful.[3] God is calling us to his own character, and, thus, his own faithfulness. In scripture, to have genuine faith is always manifest in determined faithfulness.

Biblical faith—faith as God defines it—is much more than most may think. It is priceless and beautiful and lofty. It is all encompassing and all-powerful "if you have faith as small as a mustard seed..."[4] The faith that I possess is what possesses me. It is the victory that overcomes the world.[5] It is not just a small, single, dull, flat stone; it is an enormous, intricate, sparkling, three-faceted gem!

Faith's first facet is the most basic and is often seen by at least some as all that faith is. It is an acceptance of the truth of who Jesus is—the Lord and Savior, the Messiah, the Christ, Emmanuel, the Son of God, the Son of Man. It is the mental ascent to the truth of Jesus's identity as the Christ, the Son of God.[6] We must believe in the reality of the message before we can come to trust in its implications. God loves us all and wills that whoever believes in Christ not be condemned.[7] To not believe in Christ, however, will ultimately prove disastrous: "If you do not believe that I am he, you will indeed die in your sins."[8] Believing Jesus is who he claimed to be is the first facet of the gem.

The second facet is our response to our mental ascent—it is our own personal surrender of faith to the reality that Jesus, the Lord and Savior, is to be *our* Lord and our God.[9] It is when our conviction concerning Christ supercedes and supplants all our idols. There are many things that we may to some degree believe, but that we do nothing about and that have little or no effect on us. Many are the people who claim to believe in Christ as the Son of God but whose lives reflect little to none of him. In this regard, Jesus once posed a rhetorical question about why some would dare call him "Lord" but then not bother to do what he asked of them.[10] Each of us should ask ourselves: Do I perhaps call him "Lord," but, in direct contradiction, pay little heed to his calls and commands? Christ said there would be many apparently active and involved Christians who, at judgment, would find that they had never come to know him in actuality, or at least whom Christ had never come to know.[11] He has made our truly knowing him a requisite to his truly knowing us. And our supposed knowing of him, without his actual knowing of us, will always prove useless and thus disastrous!

The third faith facet is living a life of surrender. "'But my righteous one will live by faith. And I take no pleasure in the one who shrinks back.' But we do not belong to those who shrink back and are destroyed, but to those who have faith and are saved."[12] The one who believes in the reality of Christ as Lord and Savior and even initially surrenders his life to him but then "shrinks back" cannot be said to have "lived by faith." They may have had a faith moment—that moment of ascent. They may have had a faith surrender-experience—that moment where one accepts Jesus as Lord and Savior. But it is only in living a life fully by faith that one can truly claim to have a saving faith. A too-shallow and partial faith in reality only accepts Jesus as the savior; a deep and full faith accepts him not only as a personal savior, but as the personal Lord.

Paul said at the end of his arduous but faithful ministry life, "I have fought the good fight. I have finished the race. *I have kept the faith.*"[13] Faith must be kept. Genuine faith will finish stronger than it started. Faith must become a possession for life and not only to be had for just a while. Be faithful even to the point of death, and you will be given a crown of life.[14]

In rehearsing his ministry to the Corinthians, in a letter to them, Paul wrote,

> Now, brothers and sisters, I want to remind you of the gospel I preached to you, which you received and on which you have taken your stand. By this gospel, you are saved if you hold firmly to the word I preached to you. Otherwise, you have believed in vain.[15]

Reception of the gospel—the complete three-faceted faith described in scripture—involves, as Paul explains, receiving the gospel as truth ("you received"), taking a stand on it and committing to it ("on which you have taken your stand"), and holding firmly to it for life ("hold firmly to the word"). Any other expression of faith is, at best, incomplete and, as Paul calls it, "in vain." In other words, it is useless. James too calls faith without commensurate action dead.[16]

As members of Christ's church—the bride of Christ—we are called not just to engagement (coming to believe he is the one for us, so to speak). We are called not only to an engagement culminating in a marriage ceremony (believing and surrendering). Rather we are called to the fullness of all three—an engagement, a marriage, and then a life of faithful partnership. The most beautiful testimony to the faithfulness of marriage, as God designed it, is not in how it starts off, in a romance, an enchanting engagement, and a lovely wedding, but in how it survives, thrives, and ends! A joyful fiftieth or seventy-fifth wedding anniversary is much more celebration worthy than a marriage ceremony could ever be, no matter how much time energy and money can be spent on such a beginning.

"Be faithful, even to the point of death, and I will give you life as your victor's crown."[14]

Either finish or be finished.

Inspiration: Author Nicholas Sparks wrote the sentimental, moving book *The Notebook* based on the lives and marriage of his wife's grandparents, whom he observed acting as loving, doting newlyweds to the very end.[17] A later movie based on the book depicts an older couple at the end of life.[18] The wife has Alzheimer's and cannot remember who her husband is. At the start of her dementia, she had written down their original love story and how it all started, telling him to read it to her as she disappeared into dementia, and she would "come back to him." After she then mentally drifted away for some time, she becomes lucid, remembering who he is for a time, before lapsing back into her mental darkness. During her time of lucidity, he assures her he will never leave her but will stay with her until the end.

Finally, in a moving scene, they express their undying love for the other and fall asleep together in her nursing home bed. A nurse finds them the next morning having died peacefully in bed together. Although this story is only about enduring human faithfulness and love, biblical faith in God works even more powerfully through the love God gives us. The apostle Paul says, "The only thing that counts is faith expressing itself through love."[19] True faith in God is enduring faith because it is not first based on temporal emotion and sentiment, but rather it is based on reality and reason. Biblical love (*agape*, Greek) is also not based on emotion and sentiment, but it is based on the character of God to simply do what is right toward him and others, regardless of how one might feel. Thus, faithful love between two godly people demonstrates both the faith in and love for God that should exist in all believers. The storyline of the aforementioned movie movingly demonstrates the three-faceted design of God for human marriage—accepting that the one you love will be your lifelong mate (acceptance), making the marital commitments and vows (surrender), and living faithfully for life together (lifelong fidelity in all its facets).

Because of who and what he is, God wants each of us to experience such a faithful and loving relationship with him, both in this life and then with him forever in eternity.

Prayer: Father, help me to have a complete faith in you, expressed in a complete love for you—a faith and love that doesn't just start with you and what I can receive from you, but finishes in all I can give back to you. Guide me to finish stronger than I began. May your faithfulness grow in me as I grow in you. May my faith, rather than proving vain, bear fruit for you until the return of Christ.

Reflection: How strong and enduring is my faith and love for Christ? Describe the three facets of your own faith. Describe why beginning without ending is tragic.

References:
1. Matt. 13:44–46.
2. Eph. 1:18.
3. Ps. 36:5.
4. Matt. 17:20.
5. 1 John 5:4.
6. John 20:31.
7. John 3:16; 1 Tim. 2:4.
8. John 8:24.
9. John 20:28.
10. Luke 6:46.
11. Matt. 7:22–23.
12. Heb. 10:38–29; Hab. 2:4; Rom. 1:17.
13. 2 Tim. 4:7.

14. Rev. 2:10.
15. 1 Cor. 15:1–2.
16. James 2:17.
17. Nicholas Sparks, *The Notebook*, New York: Warner Books, 1996.
18. Cassavetes, Nick, *The Notebook* [Motion picture], United States: Warner Brothers, 2004.
19. Gal. 5:6.

15

These Three Remain: Faith, Hope, and Love[1]

Faith, hope, and love are the preeminent and most enduring of virtues and gifts in the here and now. But only love transcends this age, because it is the essence of God himself.[2] Faith is to be all encompassing in this life. Our faith will ultimately define us, for it is what we believe about God, the cosmos, ourselves, and others, as well as the purpose behind all of it. Faith is the conviction that drives who we are and how we live. Hope flows from faith, because hope is the expectation of what is to come. Biblical hope is contrary to the modern idea. The modern idea of hope means to wish something to happen. Biblical hope means to expect it to happen based on what is believed.

Many see miracles as the preeminent gifts—healings, prophecy, exorcisms, speaking in tongues, and so forth. But perhaps what we call "miracles" are not really miracles at all. Perhaps they are only faith's ability within us to tap into what has always been possible: "Truly I tell you, if you have faith as small as a mustard seed, you can say to this mountain, 'Move from here to there,' and it will move. Nothing will be impossible for you."[3]

Maybe some miracles are not God actually intervening and causing a thing to happen, but because we simply trust God's having said we *could* do it, we can then do it by the power he has already put in us.[4] Perhaps we are like fearful children whose parents convince them they can do something, such as ride a bike. Children don't first do the difficult thing because they believe in themselves, but because they believe in their parents or teachers. The innate ability to do such things is already there though, inherited from the parents themselves. Children believe in their parents because the parents believe in their children. Children also trust their parents because their parents not only encourage them to do it, but because their parents are there to steady the children as they begin, to keep their children from danger and hard falls. They are, as well, there to care for and comfort when falls occur.

It is the same with believers and our heavenly Father. He tells us we can do a seemingly impossible thing, and then he tells us he will be there with us: "Therefore go and make disciples of all nations...and teaching them to obey everything I have commanded you. And surely I am with you always, to the very end of the age."[5] The apostle Paul knew this personally and experientially: "At my first defense, no one came to my support, but everyone deserted me...But the Lord stood at my side and gave me strength, so that, through me, the message might be fully proclaimed and all the Gentiles might hear it. And I was delivered from the lion's mouth."[6] God does not promise us that he will keep us *from* all challenges and harms. When necessary, he actually might even lead us, for good purpose, into into harm's way. He does, however, promise to lead and guide us *through* challenge and harm. But he never asks more of us than he asked of himself when he came in human form to live and die for us. And his work is always for the ultimate good.

God noted the nature of our human faith potential all the way back to the crisis at Babel: "The Lord said, 'If as one people speaking the same language they have begun to do this, then nothing they plan to do will be impossible for them.'"[7] Nothing is impossible for them. Hmm. Even in their diversion from the will of God, humanity was still capable of doing seemingly impossible things! History has proven that there are always things that many assume are impossible or at least never even dreamed of but that are ultimately shown to be quite possible. Some prove to be wonderful, such as vaccinations. On the other hand, some things humanity has invented and done have proved nothing short of tragic, such as the invention and production of hydrogen bombs. Thus, God often intervenes to guide, prevent, protect, and sometimes chasten us in our human endeavors.

Humans are blessed from conception, because at the least, we are all greatly gifted as God's image-bearers.[8] Scripture tells us that also all of the truly good gifts come from God.[9] They always have, and they always will. And from early on, God has given humans the capacity to do amazingly miraculous things. For example, Moses was the lightning rod for ten supernatural, calamitous plagues that God brought on Egypt in order to free his people, Israel, from their bondage in Egypt.[10]

The Bible promised early on that God ultimately would pour out his Spirit on "all flesh"—people from all demographics—and it came about at the first Pentecost commemoration after Christ's return to heaven.[11] Luke reveals through the Book of Acts, spanning about thirty-five years, loosely from around 30 AD to around 65 AD, a cadre of miracles performed by the apostles and prophets of Christ. People spoke in languages ("tongues") they had never learned, the sick were healed, the dead were raised, prison doors were miraculously opened, demons were cast out, and so on.

This set in motion the distribution of a number of specially assigned gifts to various disciples. Some of these would normally be seen as miraculous—healing, miraculous powers, prophecy, distinguishing between spirits, speaking in and interpreting tongues, and the like. Others would certainly seem to be more innate talents and abilities, such as wisdom, knowledge, and faith, but in these cases they were given directly by the Spirit.[12] As the various churches were established and their members grew in the faith, more functional gifts would emerge, such as serving, teaching, encouraging, and giving.[13]

Thus, when Paul wrote the Corinthian church about the uses and abuses of their spiritual gifts, he took pause in the middle of it to explain to them what the greatest and most enduring gifts of all are—faith, hope, and love. By inference, it may be assumed that not all of the church members had one of the miraculous gifts.[14] However, every single person who would be saved and become a part of Christ's church are, in fact, *required* to have the gift of faith in him. And our faith is what produces hope in us. Hope (*elpis,* Greek) is what is fully expected to happen.[15]

Only through this biblical faith in God can the love God commands and the love Paul discusses with the Corinthians ever be expressed.[16] Paul describes the link from faith to hope to the Roman church, saying,

> Therefore, since we have been justified through faith, we have peace with God through our Lord Jesus Christ, through whom we have gained access by faith into this grace in which we now stand. And we boast in the hope of the glory of God. Not only so, but we also glory in our sufferings, because we know that suffering produces perseverance; perseverance, character; and character, hope. And hope does not put us to shame because God's love has been poured out into our hearts through the Holy Spirit, who has been given to us.[17]

It all begins and ends with faith, "from first to last," "from beginning to end," "from faith to faith."[18] Without faith, one cannot even connect with God, let alone be pleasing to him.[19] Anything that we do that is not done out of faith in God is, in fact, of sin.[20]

Paul, in the scripture quoted above, explains to us that faith begins a chain of developments beginning with the inevitable challenges and suffering that produce perseverance. Then, perseverance brings character growth. This Christ-like character is what produces the hope that only God can inspire—the full and real expectation that God can and will fulfill all his promises to us in Christ.

However, it is only love, rather than faith and hope, that never ends, because love is the very essence of God himself, and it will, in the end, be our own essence in the kingdom of Heaven.

Faith is love's essential precursor, and hope completely changes us into new creations with new identities and expectancies. But love makes us like God. And when we are in the presence of God, faith and hope will no longer exist, because we will no longer need them.

Thus faith, hope, and love are the greatest and most enduring gifts of God to his "new" humanity—the church. They are the preeminent spiritual gifts that all the other spiritual gifts were given to foster and develop. When Jesus returns, and he finally and completely establishes the fullness of the kingdom of God with us, faith and hope will be needed no more because faith is the substance of what we hope for, and what we presently hope for will have been realized then. When Christ returns, we will no longer walk by faith, but we will instead finally walk by "sight," because, "then we shall see face to face."[21]

Eagerly desire these, the highest of gifts—faith and hope, and God will then show you the most excellent way—the way of love![22]

Inspiration: In 1995, Mary Ann Franco was injured in a car accident and completely lost her vision. For the next twenty-one years, she would live that way, unable to even see her grandchildren. In the spring of 2016, Mary suffered another accident, falling in her home and suffering an injury to her spine, which required surgery. On April 6, she woke up from the surgery able to see again! Even prior to losing her eyesight, she had already been color-blind, yet she woke up, not only able to see, but able to see the full array of colors. Medical explanations were proposed, but her own neurosurgeon—a scientist—said on network news, "It's a true miracle." Miracles happen—the unlikely, the unbelievable. Similarly, we all go through our own accidents that disconnect us from God and cast us into spiritual darkness. When we come to Christ though, a miracle of God happens within us, and not only can we see again, but we can also see better than we ever could before. We have conviction. We have real hope. When Christ finally returns and redeems us, we will at that time see better than we can imagine: "For now we see only a reflection as in a mirror; then we shall see face to face. Now I know in part; then I shall know fully, even as I am fully known."[23] Yes, when we come to Christ, we end up seeing better than ever. And when Christ returns, we will see everything completely and clearly. But in the meantime, it turns out pretty good here. Enjoy.

Prayer: Father, help me to savor and fully experience the enduring gifts given to all believers—faith, hope, and love. Grow and strengthen my faith, increase my hope, and expand and deepen my love.

Reflection: How do I see faith, hope, and love growing within me? How might it be that what are seen as miracles are just unrecognized abilities of those who truly believe? Why are we often afraid of miracles?

References:
1. 1 Cor. 13:13.
2. 1 John 4:8.
3. Matt. 17:20.
4. Eph. 3:20–21; Phil 4:13.
5. Matt. 28:19–20.
6. 2 Tim. 4:16–17.
7. Gen. 11:6.
8. Ps. 139:14.
9. James 1:17.
10. Ex. 7–12.
11. Joel 2:28–23; Acts 2:16–21.
12. 1 Cor. 12:8–10.
13. Rom. 12:6–8.
14. 1 Cor. 12:29–30.
15. *Vine's Complete Expository Dictionary of Old and New Testament Words.* W. Vine, M. F. Unger, and W. White. Nashville: Thomas Nelson, 1984.
16. Gal. 5:6; 1 Pet. 1:22; 1 Cor. 13:4–7.
17. Rom. 5:1–5.

18. Rom. 1:17.
19. Heb. 11:6.
20. Rom. 14:23.
21. 1 Cor. 13:12.
22. 1 Cor. 12:31.
23. 1 Cor. 13:12.

16

Faith Is Our Shield Against Doubt and Fear

In our Christian walk, evil will come upon us all early and often. Satan will not leave us uncontested. He is the tempter and the tester. There is a power behind those things that stand between us and God and that potentially damage and even destroy us. The evil forces of this present dark world still possess unimaginable power. The apostle Paul even referred to Satan as " the god of this age."[1] Although Satan is not God's equal, he is indeed his most powerful enemy. Satan is not omnipresent, but he is ever-present. And he apparently has a wicked and destructive force of fallen, evil angels and demons bent on our destruction.[2] Just as we might encounter angels and be unaware of it, so it might be with evil spirits.[3] The scriptures have many accounts of various kinds of encounters with Satan and evil spirits. Because of the fear of others' reactions, stories of modern day evil encounters are often discussed only in private. However, the annals of Christian history up until now continue to give accounts of the reality of evil's continuing work in this present age against the people of God and the world in general, both individually and collectively.

None of us are immune. Apart from God, all of us are exposed to varying degrees. Only in Christ does a shield exist. Be assured, that shield is the faith God gives us.

After his baptism, even Jesus was severely tested by Satan in the wilderness.[4] The world is our "wilderness" and life is our own test. Satan is our accuser. He is the prince of darkness. He is a thief. He is the destroyer. And believers have "prices on our heads," so to speak, in the spiritual realm.[5] Thus, we must not be unaware of the devil's schemes against us.[6] Satan and his demonic forces set traps along our paths, and we must be wary of them or we will be ensnared. Satan is as a "roaring lion" seeking to devour us at any possible time.[7]

We are not, however, defenseless. The Spirit of God within us is much more powerful than the Evil One without.[8] Paul wrote to the Ephesian church about the spiritual battle we face against the evil world of darkness, saying,

> Finally, be strong in the Lord and in his mighty power. Put on the full armor of God, so that you can take your stand against the devil's schemes. For our struggle is not against flesh and blood, but against the rulers, against the authorities, against the powers of this dark world and against the spiritual forces of evil in the heavenly realms. Therefore, put on the full armor of God, so that when the day of evil comes, you may be able to stand your ground and, after you have done everything, to stand.[9]

Although I'm sure Satan would surely have us think otherwise, our battle is not merely a human one. Rather our battle is against the forces of evil working out of another realm—the heavenly or spiritual realm. And these evil powers are more powerful than we are in our present human state. But their power is not greater than God's! Therefore, our strength must be in the Lord and not in ourselves. It is God alone that gives us power over evil.[10] The "day of evil" will surely come to each of us; Satan will most assuredly have his days with us. But we can withstand him through Christ. We can withstand him *only* through Christ.

God gives each of us a spiritual armor. It is a full person, battle-tested protection against evil. And we must wear the whole thing—to "put on the full armor of God"—to be properly prepared. It all begins and ends with our faith in God—the shield of faith, Paul calls it. We must "be strong in the Lord and in his mighty power"! Our strength against Satan will certainly not be found in ourselves. Ever! Not even once.

> Stand firm, then, with the belt of truth buckled around your waist, with the breastplate of righteousness in place, and with your feet fitted with the readiness that comes from the gospel of peace. In addition to all this, take up the shield of faith, with which you can extinguish all the flaming arrows of the evil one. Take the helmet of salvation and the sword of the Spirit, which is the word of God. And pray in the Spirit on all occasions with all kinds of prayers and requests. With this in mind, be alert and always keep on praying for all the Lord's people.[11]

There is a belt of truth, a breastplate of righteousness, protective shoes from the gospel of peace, a helmet of salvation, and a sword of the Spirit. There is also the all-important shield of faith.

The belt is what holds it all together. This belt of our armor is the truth. Jesus is the truth. He is what holds it all together. The truth is who he is, what he is, and what he wills for us and for his kingdom. The truth is simply that: the truth. It is unchanging because it emanates from the very nature of the ever-existent God who never changes.

There is also a breastplate of righteousness. The breastplate protects the heart and the vital internal organs. There are three kinds of "righteousness" mentioned in scripture, one the wrong kind and two right kinds. The first is "self-righteousness." It is the malady caused by the fruit of the Tree of the Knowledge of Good and Evil. It is the arrogant delusions of legalism—that we are "right because we are 'right'." Secondly, there is the "righteousness from God" that is based on the reality that we are viewed by him as right "because he is right."[12] It is the righteousness that is gifted to us by God's grace through our faith in his rightness and goodness and by our renouncing any claim to a righteousness of our own.[13]

The third righteousness is subsequent to the second. It is not about receiving grace; it is about giving grace. It is not to somehow "earn" grace because that is impossible; it is because grace has been freely given to us. It is about graceful living. We freely give what has been freely given us. It is about faithfully seeking to live aright in Christ because of our love for and trust in him. It is not the source of our salvation; it is the result of our salvation.[14] It is about good and right living in imitation of Christ. It is not where we put our faith; our faith is only in him. It is the fruit of our faith. It is what Jesus's teaching in the Sermon on the Mount is all about—graceful living.[15]

As an important part of the armor, there are the protective shoes. As stated in the above text, they are fitted with the "readiness that comes from the gospel of peace." These are our hybrid army boots and running shoes. But our fight is not one of conquest; it is a war of peace fought with the proclamation of the gospel of peace. We are on a mission, and we must be ready always to move decisively and forcefully in the advancement of our mission as peacemakers. We are ambassadors of the kingdom of God; we are soldiers in the almighty army of God, the army fighting for peace.[16] We, therefore, are not soldiers in the human army, and the weapons we fight with are not the same weapons the world fights with.[17]

Next is the helmet of salvation. The helmet protects the head and the brain—the mind. It also bears the insignia of whose we are—our seal; whoever wins our mind wins the battle within us. We are either conformed to the world by our minds or transformed by God through our minds.[18] Our minds are renewed by the sanctifying work of the Holy Spirit, and this holiness must be protected from evil's deceptive attacks on our thinking. We must love God with all of our minds.[19] To do this, we must set our minds on things above.[20] And we must take our thoughts captive and make them obedient to Christ.[21] We must focus our minds on things that are excellent and praiseworthy not on thoughts that are useless or counterproductive to the kingdom of God.[22]

The one weapon that is not only defensive but can be offensive is the sword of the Holy Spirit of God. And it is the word of God. We have an armor, and we must be armed. Our offensive, however, is not a destructive attack; it is one of constructive recovery and redemption. It is not an attack of war; it is the advancement of peace. It is not a war of conquest; it is a war of surrender. It is not a war against anything, in fact; it is a war for something. And it penetrates hearts, not to destroy them, but in order to save them. The word of God is thus said to be sharper than any double-edged sword, and it cuts deeply and lays the human heart open for God's inspection and reconstructive healing.[23]

The last part of the spiritual armor that Paul describes in the above text is the shield of faith. In the kind of ancient battles Paul was referring to, ones that required armor, a strongly constructed and well-wielded shield was critical to survival. And the shield of faith is critical to our own spiritual survival. With it, we can "extinguish the flaming arrows of the evil one." Satan's arrows are toxic, poison-tipped, and razor sharp. And they are aflame. They are deadly and destructive. They seek out the cracks and seams in our armors—any crevice or hole that might be vulnerable. Thus, we need this shield to protect the most vulnerable but essential parts of our armament.

Faith is our shield against fears, doubts, reservations, insecurities, accusations, guilt, shame, and temptations. These fiery darts will be directed at our weaknesses, and we must be actively fending them off with our shield, lest they find a weakness in our armor. This shield is made of hard, burnished steel that is our deep, abiding, substantive, decisive faith conviction about the reality of the truth of Christ. It is the shield that protects us against the lies that can deceive and destroy us, robbing us of the life of God.

But with Christ's armor, we will prove to be "more than conquerors."[24] The forces of the evil one were defeated in Christ's death, burial, and resurrection. The mop-up action is to be completed by God's Holy Spirit working through Christ's holy people, the church. Our fight for peace must be resolute and determined. We must ever be strong and confident in who Christ is and what he accomplished for us, not anything we can be or do apart from him. We must be faithful—full of faith. Our faith in God is, in fact, our shield against failure and defeat.

As Paul wrote, we must be strong in the Lord and in *his* mighty power. Because Jesus indeed is Lord!

Inspiration: Our armor of God can be thought of as a Star Wars type of force field that emanates from a Spirit-filled heart. King David of Israel was said to have had this kind of heart; in fact, he was said to have had a heart like God's.[25] Many a young child has been awed by the story of David's gallantry in the story found in 1 Samuel, when as a young shepherd boy, he bravely defeated the Philistine giant, Goliath.[26] The fierce giant was said to have been nearly ten feet tall, worn a 125-pound armor, and carried a spear with an iron tip weighing fifteen pounds! In addition, being a leading soldier, he also had his own personal shield bearer in front of him.

The armies of Philistia and Israel were in a standoff, with only a valley separating them. Goliath had been coming out for forty days, taunting the army of God with arrogant and fierce challenges. Then one day, David showed up, having been sent by his father, Jesse, to bring food and to check up on his brothers. David was just a young shepherd boy and had only recently become a lowly shield bearer of his own King Saul. Unbeknownst even to Saul though, David had already been chosen and anointed as the next king, which had been done by Samuel the prophet at God's direction. While near the battle-front, David heard Goliath's offenses and challenges and, after some inquiry, said he would surely take on this pagan giant. David had become an expert at using his slingshot, fighting and killing lions and bears that had attacked his sheep. David said, "The Lord who rescued me from the paw of the lion and the paw of the bear will rescue me from the hand of this Philistine."[27] Ignoring the cynical scoffing of his older brother, David was taken to Saul, whom he was able to convince to let him go out to face Goliath. In an act of cowardice on the king's part, Saul prepared the young boy for battle, putting his own tunic on David and fitting him with a coat of armor and a helmet. However, David, having never worn such, said he would forego the armor and simply fight as he had as a shepherd. His faith would be his shield! As David proceeded alone by his faith in God, Goliath, preceded by his shield bearer, began to ridicule and curse the smaller, much younger David in the name of the Philistine gods. David, however, stood strong, saying,

> You come against me with sword and spear and javelin, but I come against you in the name of the Lord Almighty, the God of the armies of Israel, whom you have defied. This day, the Lord will deliver you into my hands, and I'll strike you down and cut off your head. This very day, I will give the carcasses of the Philistine army to the birds and the wild animals, and the whole world will know that there is a God in Israel. All those gathered here will know that it is not by sword or spear that the Lord saves; for the battle is the Lord's, and he will give all of you into our hands.[27]

Then, with a single stone picked up from the river and with his own lowly but well-worn slingshot, David approached the advancing giant. He slung one stone at Goliath, felling him with a single direct hit onto his forehead. And just that quickly, down the giant went! Goliath had come in human strength and size, wearing human armor. David fought with the full armor of God—the spiritual force field—emanating from a heart full of the Spirit and wholly devoted to God.[29] His was the very same armor that we are to wear in our spiritual battles. Its steel is not earthly but heavenly. Its shield is not a shield of steel, but a shield of faith in the Almighty God of heaven and earth. James said that if we, as Christians, will resist Satan, the giant who still taunts God's army, this evil giant will, in fact, run from us.[30] "For the battle is not ours, but God's."[31] And he is, and will remain, undaunted and undefeated! If we advance the fight through his power, so will we be undefeated!

Prayer: Father, help me to put on your full armor that I may be able to stand against our ultimate foe, Satan, on the evil days of his attacks. Please let me be fearless in faith, doubtless in courage, and deft in spiritual battle. Let your sword of the Spirit—your word—be powerful in my hands in advancing your kingdom in the face of his fierce opposition and destructive intent. May my shield against evil ever and only be my faith in you, O Holy God.

Reflection: Do I wear the full and complete armor of God—every part of it? Where might the weaknesses in my armor be that Satan can exploit? Am I ready for when the evil day comes to my life, and if not, what must I do to become ready? Consider again carefully each part of the ancient armor and its spiritual correlate to our own armors as Christians.

References:
1. 2 Cor. 4:4.
2. Eph. 6:12; 1 Pet. 5:8
3. Heb. 13:2.
4. Matt. 4:1.
5. Eph. 1:13.
6. 2 Cor. 2:11.
7. 1 Pet. 5:8.
8. 1 John 4:4.
9. Eph. 6:10–13.
10. Mark 3:15.
11. Eph. 6:14–18.
12. Rom. 1:17.
13. Rom. 4:3–5.
14. Eph. 2:8–10.
15. Matt. 5–7.
16. 2 Cor. 5:20.
17. 2 Cor. 10:4.
18. Rom. 12:1–2.
19. Matt. 22:37.
20. Col. 3:2.
21. 2 Cor. 10:4–5.

22. Phil. 4:8.
23. Heb. 4:12–13.
24. Rom. 8:31–39.
25. 1 Sam. 13:14; Acts 13:22.
26. 1 Sam. 17.
27. 1 Sam. 17:37.
28. 1 Sam. 17:45–47.
29. 2 Chron. 16:9.
30. James 4:7.
31. 2 Chron. 20:15.

17

Faith Is Not Merely the Key to Victory; It Is the Victory

The apostle John wrote, "This is the victory that has overcome the world, even our faith."[1] Faith is the core component of our life and spiritual survival. Faith is the basis of our relationship to God. We are, of course, justified by our faith in Christ Jesus. However, it is Christ that justifies us, not faith itself, as a stand-alone. Faith alone can do nothing. It is but an idea, a human experience. We can strongly believe things that are not true, which will always ultimately do more harm than any good that might initially come from believing untruths.

But it is God alone who forgives our sin. It is by his grace and mercy that he allows us access to him on the basis of our willingness to trust in him. All sin is, in fact, ultimately an offense to God. It is his world, his house. It is about him. He sets the house rules. We all belong to him, whether we give our lives to him or not. And one day, everyone who has ever lived will admit that Jesus is, indeed, Lord. For it will be obvious when he reveals himself at the final redemption. And it is our faith in God that activates him in us in some powerful way. It prompts him to, by an act of his own grace, call us, choose us, and justify us through the faith he sees within us—our belief in Christ as Lord and Savior and in the reality of what Christ accomplished for us.[2]

It is through our faith in him that we are united with Christ in his death, burial, and resurrection, so that we can live a new life in him, realized in our baptism into him.[3] Thus, it is by faith in Christ that we live our life in the "new way of the Spirit and not in the old way of the written code."[4] Faith is thus our work, but our justification is God's work, and God's alone![5]

Because of God's lavish grace for us, in Christ we face no condemnation at all. "Who will bring any charge against those whom God has chosen?"[6] Our accuser has been defeated and, in regard to us as believers, muted.[7] Our serpent tempter and prosecutor is without a law with which to prosecute us, because we have been set free from the law and its toxic effects on humanity.[8] And we have had, in Christ, the right restored to us to eat from the eternal, life-giving Tree of Life.[9]

Satan's accusations and attacks against us are stopped at the place where, in the muck and mire of the gulley of our pre-Christian lives, our faith meets Jesus's blood. His is the ultimate cleansing power. Jesus is able to forever and completely save those who come to and live by faith in him.[10] It is not faith in our faith itself—its substance, its strength, its tenacity. It is not faith in what we believe. It is not our faith in the rightness of all the specifics of our beliefs and doctrines or our knowledge of or our attainment in regard to them. It not our faith alone that saves us; it is our faith in Christ alone that saves us. Thus Paul summarizes our win in Christ, saying,

> No, in all these things, we are more than conquerors through him who loved us. For I am convinced that neither death nor life, neither angels nor demons, neither the present nor the future, nor any powers, neither height nor depth, nor anything else in all creation will be able to separate us from the love of God that is in Christ Jesus our Lord.[11]

We are more than conquerors because Christ has already won the battle for us—our battle. Our salvation game begins in him with the final score already on the scoreboard. Jesus wins! So I win through him. For our part in Christ, there is no scorekeeper and we are not judged by the world's rules! We live above and beyond the rules of the fruit of the knowledge of good and evil that can only poison us. For the believer, the game is over before any end game can begin.

God is completely just, meaning that God is fair and righteous in all he says and does. It is his nature, and his character is unchanging. He reconciles everything. In his infinite power and wisdom, he designed and created it all for this purpose. And he will complete his work, with me or without me. Ultimately, he makes everything and everyone balance out. Those that seek "rewards" in this life will not get them in the next, as seen in Jesus's story of the rich man and the begger named Lazarus. We read in Jesus's story, "But Abraham replied, 'Son, remember that in your lifetime, you received your good things, while Lazarus received bad things, but now he is comforted here, and you are in agony.'"[12] One had it good in this life and got nothing in the next. The other got little here but was rewarded in the next. It all balances out in the end. God is just; he is fair. He exists only according to his own essence and nature—his rules.

Humanity is simply and in general not very just though. Society is often not really very fair. Individuals apart from God become narcissistic and self-centered. It all becomes about the almight "me." It started with the curse on the woman in the story of the first sin in the Garden of Eden. God told the woman, "Your desire will be for your husband, and he will rule over you." Understood in its likely deeper metaphorical sense and implications, this tells us that in a sinful world, the stronger will dominate the weaker, the richer will dominate the poorer, the majority will dominate the minority, and so forth.[13] Those who are down will, more often than not, not be picked up by those standing, but rather they will be stepped on and abased. In this present age, there will always be an ongoing battle for dominance. Satan started it, and the curse itself continues it. Narcicissm is rampant in our world. It's not new, but it finds fertile soil in arrogant hearts with the rotting compost of the sense of entitlement tilled deeply into it. In an example in the life of God's Old Testament people, Israel, and which has been replicated over and over, socially and culturally, through the ages, we read,

> Jeshurun [Israel] grew fat and kicked; filled with food, they became heavy and sleek. They abandoned the God who made them and rejected the Rock their Savior. They made him jealous with their foreign gods and angered him with their detestable idols. They sacrificed to false gods, which are not God—gods they had not known, gods that recently appeared, gods your ancestors did not fear. You deserted the Rock, who fathered you; you forgot the God who gave you birth.[14]

Each generation must recognize its unique and modern version of this same old human exalting, self-centered, narcisstic philosophy. Satan has no new tricks. He convinces each generation that they are "like God" and worthy of being served, worthy of domination, and worthy of self-determination. He convinces us that we can be good and right by our own device and effort, and that it is okay to compete with and ultimately dominate others because of our inherent "rights" to do so! Society at large has long been ruled by it. Neither are Christianity or religion in general immune to its toxic effects.

Seeds of human-centeredness are planted in all churches and doctrines. Seekers of truth must constantly be rigorous and alert in prayer to allow the Spirit to work inwardly in us with the word. We must be ready and willing for him to continually excise from us the curse of "weeds," that resulted from the first sin and which drives us to have to labor for rightness on our own. And as with all of the Deceiver's schemes, they begin with a thread of truth, but then wind their way to fallacy, and finally, to opposing God in the sometimes subtle and often not-so-subtle exaltation of ourselves. Modern humanism clearly believes and states that humanity no longer has the "need" for belief in God, as if the truth is a choice we merely fabricate and not the reality that we must seek and discover.

The battle for dominance that began in the Garden of Eden continues still, even in the freedom-loving Western civilizations of the twenty-first century. "Freedom and justice for all" is in reality an illusion. "That all men are created equal" is a self-evident reality that is rarely applied among sinful people both in and out of God's church. Perhaps under the present curse, it is impossible it is supposed. The wealthy and privileged often do not get what they deserve, but rather what they want. Many live gross, decadent lives, often flaunting the law, living behind a wall of high-paid lawyers and insider connections. They get privileges and comforts they often have not worked for at all. They get undeserved pleasures, privileges, and comforts, and they most often do not receive the just punishment of the law poor people are subjected to.

On the other hand, the poor must often face busy, emotionless judges behind the pleas of overworked and unmotivated public defenders, who are often forced to represent them for less than they could otherwise be making. The wealthy go free after committing felonies. The poor rot in jail over misdemeanors. Humanity is not fair—it never has been and, in its fallen state, is incapable of truly being so. The rich dominate and take advantage of the poor. The poor seemingly reciprocate by hating, harassing, and stealing from the rich at every opportunity. The majority takes advantage of the minority, and the minority strikes back with resentment, hatred, and vitriol. The strong dominate the weak, and the weak hit back with subterfuge. Men control women, and women fight back with their own strengths and abilities, feeling justified to hate, hit, and hurt because of the subjugation that has beset them.

However, only hate prevails when anyone tries to prevail over anyone else. It is the curse, the noxious fruit of the Tree of the Knowledge of Good and Evil. But, it is not this way in the shade of the Tree of Life, which to us is Jesus Christ! Under its (his) branches and enjoying its lifegiving fruit, humankind can feed on that which causes us to live aright, to love others unselfishly, to esteem others better than ourselves, to go the extra mile, to lend freely without expecting anything in return, and so forth. We can do it, if we only will, because the God of grace gives us all we need, including his own Spirit, and we can trust him completely. We don't trust he will give us all we want. God forbid such a curse! We trust that he will give us all we need. And only he knows what that even is!

God is fair and just. Always. It is clearly stated in scripture, "God is just: He will pay back trouble to those who trouble you and give relief to you who are troubled, and to us as well."[15] Each of us can bank on it—God will ultimately prove to be fair to us and to everyone else as well. "For God will bring every deed into judgment, including every hidden thing, whether it is good or evil."[16] Nothing will escape his purview and subsequent judgment. Jesus said, "I tell you that everyone will have to give account on the Day of Judgment for every empty word they have spoken."[17] For those still fettered by the curse of sin, he will judge every single idle word, and he doesn't miss a thing. Our only hope is Christ. No one can come to God except through him.[18]

Believers, however, have been released from the cursed purview of the law and thus will not be judged by it.[19] The unbeliever will face the judge, God, alone and at the hands of an evil prosecutor, Satan, the Accuser, who carries a daunting and impossible set of laws by which to charge violators. We must come to the reality of how the haunting Christian hymn expresses it,

> Just as I am, without one plea
> But that Thy blood was shed for me
> And that Thou bid'st me come to Thee
> O Lamb of God, I come! I come[20]

Without Christ as my defender, my best plea is "no contest." But still, without Christ, the verdict concerning me is only and always "guilty as charged."

But in Christ, God declares those who believe as already just or justified. Justification is what Christ does for us. It is a legal term meaning "to declare one as right or reasonable" and thus it equates to an acquittal of sorts. In ancient times and in certain societies, justification was the way wealthy or important people could pay their way out of charges against them. The poor however could afford no such thing, and heavy dues were thus extracted from their already-meager pay. Of course, often they could not pay and were thus imprisoned for their offenses. A sinful world will never dole out fairness. Just a bit of research in a large courthouse will demonstrate it. On the other hand, God is always and only fair. God justifies us as his people in response to our faith in his justice and mercy, not according to our ability to pay our way out with money or favors.

"Justice" is really not very different today than it has ever been, even in the freedom-loving Western world. In the fallen world, freedom is costly. Our freedom as believers cost Jesus Christ his life. The wealthy, because of their means, enjoy more freedom than the poor. Also, the poor of Western societies often enjoy certain freedoms the poor of the rest of the world do not enjoy, because of the work of others who often gave their lives in defense of the rights of the weakest among us. In reality, in virtually all societies, the well-to-do and powerful live by various kinds of "justice" systems, while the poor and disadvantaged live by "injustice" systems. Jesus cared for and looked out for the interests of the poor and calls us as his followers to do similarly.

But there's no way any of us can pay our own way out of the dilemma we face with God under the present curse of sin. But Christ has already paid for our redemption and each of us is responsible for seeking him out to receive our free gift.

The apostle Paul summarizes for us the results of our, as believers, being justified: "Therefore, there is now no condemnation for those who are in Christ Jesus, because through Christ Jesus, the law of the Spirit who gives life has set you free from the law of sin and death."[21]

Thus, as the John the apostle summarized it, "This is the victory that has overcome the world, even our faith."[22] Amen.

Repent, change your mind, and believe the gospel!

Inspiration: There are countless stories of those who have overcome great odds to win simply because they believed—they had faith in God, faith in themselves, or faith in others. The book of Hebrews lists many such individuals from Bible accounts. A simple search on the Internet will give countless historical examples. One simple but powerful example was recently reported by Michael Harthorne in a Newser article.[23] Anaya Ellis, a first grader at Greenbriar Christian Academy in Virginia, won an award in a national handwriting contest. Winning a national award is no small feat for anyone, but it was more than a simple victory for Anaya, for Anaya was born with no hands and uses no prosthetics. Her parents were obviously at first worried about her, but were reported to now be "inspired by her." In the article her mother is quoted as saying, "She ties her shoes, she gets dressed by herself; she doesn't really need any assistance to do anything." Anaya writes standing with the pencil between her two arm stubs, bending to get at the right angle. Although the award was for children with disabilities, her teacher said she was one of the best writers in the entire class. Hartorne quotes the school principal's description of Anaya: "She does not let anything get in the way of doing what she has set out to do." Jesus himself summarized the underlying faith principle, saying, "Everything is possible for one who believes."[24] And the apostle Paul wrote, "I can do all this through him who gives me strength."[25] Indeed, faith is the victory—the victory that overcomes the world. But you must believe it to experience it!

Prayer: Father, help me this day to grow in my faith. Show me how faith is, indeed, the victory that overcomes the world. Help me to live by faith and not by fear and doubt. Show me the unlimited possibilities of your power working in me and in those I love.

Reflection: How do I see faith as a victory? Why does it sometimes seem that our faith can cause us a lot of what may appear as defeat? What should be the impact on my own psyche and life when I truly believe the gospel of Christ, that I'm justified by my faith in who God is and what Christ did for me? Why do believers in Christ ultimately win and unbelievers ultimately lose?

References
1. 1 John 5:4.
2. Rom. 5:1–2.
3. Rom. 6:3–11.
4. Rom. 7:6.
5. John 6:29.
6. Rom. 8:1; 8:33.
7. Rev. 12:10.
8. Col. 2:13–15.
9. John 14:6; 11:25; Rev. 2:7.
10. Heb. 7:23–25.
11. Rom. 8:37–39.
12. Luke 16:25.
13. Gen. 3:16.
14. Deut. 32:15-18.
15. 2 Thess. 1:6–7.
16. Eccles. 12:14.
17. Matt. 12:36.
18. John 14:6.
19. Rom. 7:6; 8:1-4.
20. Charlotte Elliott, "Just as I Am," Great Britain: *Christian Remembrancer*, 1835.
21. Rom. 8:1–2.
22. 1 John 5:4.
23. Michael Harthorne, *Newser*, United States: Newser.com, 2016.
24. Mark 9:23.
25. Phil. 4:13.

18

Stand on the Side of Truth, and Move Forward without Fear

Joshua inherited the leadership of the flawed and fearful people of Israel as they completed their forty years of forced, arduous wilderness wandering. It is understandable how Jacob's descendants, as a nation born in slavery, could be flawed and fearful. Moses himself had been greatly frustrated with them, and Joshua had been Moses's assistant for much of that time, surely having grappled with the array of decisions and problems that had already been faced.

When they had first arrived in the Promised Land forty years before their final conquest, Moses sent out scouts, or spies, to check out this new land they'd only heard about and to prepare for their entry. As recorded in the story from the book of Numbers, chapters 13 and 14, it was Joshua and Caleb who were the two faithful and believing scouts among the twelve originally sent out. Although there were amazing reports about the bountiful nature of the land, the spies also reported on the fearsomeness of its inhabitants. The people of Israel listened mostly to these discouraging reports. They were frightened and longed to be back in Egypt in the relative security of their scripted lives of slavery, living again in the meager dwellings they had lived in. However, against the protests of the people, Caleb urged them, "We should go up and take possession of the land, for we can certainly do it."[1]

The nature of Joshua's and Caleb's faithful and godly responses to the unbelieving in Israel is summarized this way:

> Joshua, son of Nun, and Caleb, son of Jephunneh, who were among those who had explored the land, tore their clothes, and said to the entire Israelite assembly, "The land we passed through and explored is exceedingly good. If the Lord is pleased with us, he will lead us into that land, a land flowing with milk and honey, and will give it to us. Only do not rebel against the Lord. And do not be afraid of the people of the land because we will devour them. Their protection is gone, but the Lord is with us. Do not be afraid of them."[2]

As easily seen in their story, Joshua's and Caleb's faith was not in the power of their people to fight; their faith was in God: "He will lead us into that land" for "the Lord is with us."

Unfortunately, the people did not listen to the faithful scouts but to the fearful ones. Listening to the faithless and fearful is still the more common human reaction. Thus, God sent the people into the wilderness to wander aimlessly for forty grueling years. God had determined to rebuild the fledgling nation, and every person who was over twenty at the time of the scouts' reports was to die in the wilderness, except for Joshua and Caleb. Even Moses himself would eventually not be permitted into the Promised Land because of his own leadership failure.

Therefore, Joshua was appointed to succeed Moses and lead Israel in the conquest of the bountiful land God had promised Abraham nearly seven hundred years earlier.[3] And upon preparations to enter Canaan's land, Caleb, Joshua's faithful cohort, requested to be apportioned the formidable hill country land where the Anakites, a giant, fearsome people, lived. It was likely the best land, and Caleb still believed that, with God's help, it would be conquered.[4]

Moses's commissioning charge to Joshua, just before Joshua was to lead Israel to the conquest of the land, reads,

Be strong and courageous, for you must go with this people into the land that the Lord swore to their ancestors to give them, and you must divide it among them as their inheritance. The Lord himself goes before you and will be with you; he will never leave you nor forsake you. Do not be afraid; do not be discouraged.[5]

Then it is written, apparently as a song Moses taught Israel, "The Lord gave this command to Joshua son of Nun: 'Be strong and courageous, for you will bring the Israelites into the land I promised them on oath, and I myself will be with you.'"[6]

As Joshua then prepared to lead the nation in the conquest of the Promised Land, God said this to him:

No one will be able to stand against you all the days of your life. As I was with Moses, so I will be with you; I will never leave you nor forsake you. Be strong and courageous, because you will lead these people to inherit the land I swore to their ancestors to give them. Be strong and very courageous. Be careful to obey all the law my servant Moses gave you; do not turn from it to the right or to the left, that you may be successful wherever you go.[7]

Joshua heard and boldly followed God's instructions. In leading Israel's covenant renewal with God, this brave, devoted leader gave the people the following challenge, along with stating his own inspiring, faithful, and courageous choice:

Now fear the Lord and serve him with all faithfulness. Throw away the gods your ancestors worshiped beyond the Euphrates River and in Egypt, and serve the Lord. But if serving the Lord seems undesirable to you, then choose for yourselves this day whom you will serve, whether the gods your ancestors served beyond the Euphrates, or the gods of the Amorites, in whose land you are living. But as for me and my household, we will serve the Lord.[8]

It has been often observed that "do not be afraid," phrased in various ways, is the most repeated command in all of the scriptures. Thus, it is not so surprising to see that the "cowardly" or "fearful" will end up in destruction, as it is written, "But the cowardly, the unbelieving, the vile, the murderers, the sexually immoral, those who practice magic arts, the idolaters and all liars—they will be consigned to the fiery lake of burning sulfur. This is the second death."[9]

So, as the title of the chapter reads, "We must stand our ground on the side of truth and advance without fear." Faith is the antidote to fear. Faith is the cure for cowardice. Faith is the remedy for doubt. Faith is the key to all meaningful relationships. Faith ultimate defeats all that plagues us. Faith is the victory that overcomes the world. Faith is a decision and a determination based on valid reasoning.

On the other hand, fear is all-too-often but an emotion arising from an often-deceptive heart. Fear is the enemy of faith. Fear is a survival emotion that, rather than helping us reason and think more effectively, shuts good thinking down, triggering the "fight or flight response." Fear is often quite unreasonable. God, rather, calls us to reason it all out in advance, to come to faith, and to not give way to fear. "If God is for us, who can be against us?"[10]

Thus, biblical faith must be a reasoned faith—faith based on evidence and logic. Faith that is based on history, science, and revelation. Reasonable faith is based on truth, not on what we want to believe or what others want us to believe. Nor is it a reaction to what we do *not* want to believe or what we fear! And truth is not about what we like or what suits us or what is comfortable and safe for us. Nor is it about how we think it *should* be. Fear has no place in finding the truth because the truth can sometimes be scary to us. Fear, more often than not, ultimately obstructs our path to the truth. However, truth is just that—truth. It is reality. It is what is, and, what ultimately is, is the great "I AM"—Yahweh, the LORD. Yahweh *is*. He is the beginning and the end of all reality. He is timeless. He is the truth. All truth emanates from him. And Jesus is the exact representation of his being. Through

Jesus Christ we can behold God in human form. Jesus reveals God to us in our human format and understanding, and as well, shows us what it means for us to be truly human, the children and image bearers of God.

The scripture therefore reasons that all who stand on the side of truth, who honestly seek truth, come to Jesus.[11] Scripture also contends, clearly and simply, that "the fool says in his heart, 'There is no God.'"[12]

A person of truth must not give in to fear. Fear is about doubt. People of truth do not live by doubt but by faith—what they believe with the most certainty. Just as faith is a choice and a decision, so the emotion of fear can also lead to a wrong decision. Rather, as James wrote, "You must believe and not doubt."[13] Peter, using as an example Abraham's wife, Sarah, writes in an admonition to women, "You are her daughters if you do what is right and do not give way to fear."[14] Wow—*if you do not give way to fear*. We must not give way to doubt either.

It can be imagined how much fear was likely stirred in Sarah during her lifetime.[15] First, she was childless, and as with all women in her time, virtually her entire worth was tied up in her ability to bear children. Then, God picked her husband as his special man and had them leave their home to go to an unknown land, simply trusting the leadership of God. Further, she was allowed by her husband to be taken, not once, but twice, into the homes of powerful men—Pharaoh and Abimelech—under the guise of being Abraham's half sister (which she in fact was, but, as Abraham failed to tell them, she was also his wife).[16] Even though Abraham is called "the father of our faith," he was, just as we are, imperfect and prone to sin.

Sarah lived during hard times and lived a tough life in many ways, but she was faithful to her husband and ultimately faithful to God. Although the scriptures make it clear that neither she nor her husband were in any way perfect; they were however chosen by God for a mission. Then, centuries later, along came Peter, this Jewish Christian apostle, encouraging women to do like Sarah and not give in to fear, even when your husband might put you in such jeopardy! How much more then should we not give way to fear and doubt before God?

This first king of Israel, Saul, feared his own soldiers and disobeyed God because of it. He said to Samuel, "I have sinned. I violated the Lord's command and your instructions. I was afraid of the men and so I gave in to them."[17] He was apparently more concerned with pleasing people than pleasing God. Consequently, God sternly rejected him as king and replaced him with David.

Jesus's challenge to the apostles most assuredly applies to us all: "Peace I leave with you; my peace I give you. I do not give to you as the world gives. Do not let your hearts be troubled and do not be afraid."[18]

Jesus gives us his peace—the peace of God that surpasses human understanding.[19] Therefore, we must not let our hearts be troubled or be afraid. "God's got this." We can trust it, because we can trust him. In him we will win.

So stand your ground on the side of truth, and advance without fear!

Inspiration: Elijah is arguably the most famous of the Old Testament prophets.[20] It was he who appeared to Jesus along with Moses on the all-important Mount of Transfiguration, an incident that would signify the changing of the guard from the law-giver Moses and the Prophets to Jesus.[21] Elijah was quite unorthodox. Scary and odd are how we would likely see him, much like John the Baptist would have been seen in Jesus's time. In fact, John the Baptist was said to have been like Elijah.[22] Elijah was unquestionably God's man, though. He was best known for having to prophesy to Israel during the time of its most-wicked king, Ahab, and his perhaps even more wicked wife, Jezebel.[23] His first challenge was telling Ahab it wouldn't rain for the next few years, at least until Elijah said so. And then Elijah was sent to hide from Ahab in a ravine east of the Jordan, where he was literally fed by the ravens and drank from a brook there. The brook dried up, and he was sent to live, for a while, with a poor widow and her starving son. Next, Elijah met up with Ahab and the 450 false prophets of the idol Baal, along with 400 more prophets of the idol Asherah, to challenge them and demonstrate whose God was real and whose was not. An altar was built to Baal and another to Yahweh. The false prophets put a bull on their altar and prayed for their "god" to consume their sacrifice. In a rather humorous story, they prayed all morning and then, prompted by Elijah's taunting, prayed until evening, but all to no avail. Then, Elijah offered a bull on the altar to Yahweh and had the people drench the sacrifice and the altar, so much so that a trench was built around the altar to hold all the water. Elijah then prayed and fire came from heaven to consume not only the sacrifice, but also the wood and even the stones of the altar. And it completely dried up all of the water! Indeed, Yahweh "showed up"! Elijah and the people then executed all 850 of the deceptive false prophets Ahab and Jezebel had recruited and appointed.[24]

However, then, Elijah had to evade the wicked king and queen for a while just to keep from being killed himself. But, it was not over yet. God again sent him to face them and to prophesy of Ahab and Jezebel's impending deaths—this after Ahab and Jezebel orchestrated the completely unjust execution of a lowly Jew in order to steal his vineyard for Ahab to, of all things, plant a garden there.[25] Of course, the prophecy against them would soon come true. Finally, God took Elijah to heaven in grand style. With Elisha there to witness, a chariot and horses of fire came, and Elijah was taken up with them in some kind of whirlwind from heaven.[26] Suffice it to say, here is recorded the example a man of God who never gave way to fear, even though, at one point, in despair, he asked God to just let him die.[27]

Never ever, under any circumstance, are we, as people of God, to give way to ungodly fear. Never choose fear and doubt; choose faith instead! Trust God.

Prayer: Dear Lord, help me to never give way to ungodly fear in my life. Help me to identify and reckon with my fears. Help me to recognize when my fears stand in the way of my being and doing what my faith in you demands. May your Spirit lead and inspire me as he did Elijah.

Reflection: What in my life, in regard to God, do I fear the most? In what area or role in my life do I have the most fear? What most tends to make me doubt his existence, his character, or his will? How can I effectively address my fear and doubt challenges and move forth boldly?

References
1. Num. 13:30.
2. Num. 14:6–9.
3. Deut. 3:28; Gen. 12:1-3.
4. Josh. 14:12.
5. Deut. 31:7–8.
6. Deut. 31:22–23.
7. Josh. 1:5–7.
8. Josh. 24:14–15.
9. Rev. 21:8.
10. Rom. 8:31.
11. John 18:37; 4:23–24.
12. Ps. 14:1.
13. James 1:6.
14. 1 Pet. 3:6.
15. Gen. 12–23.
16. Gen. 12:10–20; 20:1–18.
17. 1 Sam. 15:24.
18. John 14:27.
19. Phil. 4:7.
20. 1 Kings 17–22.
21. Matt. 17:4.
22. Matt. 11:14.
23. 1 Kings 21:25–26.
24. 1 Kings 18:1–40.
25. 1 Kings 21:1–24.
26. 2 Kings 2:11–12.
27. 1 Kings 19:3–4.

19

Increase Our Faith

Faith in God is never static—either it's maturing and growing, or it's waning and dying. Faith never goes away though. The faith equation always balances to one hundred percent. As our faith in God decreases, by necessity, our faith in other things or people, as compared to trusting in God, increases. As our faith in God increases, our faith in other things or people decreases. We all live by faith, whether we like it or not; whether we want to admit it or not.

Our faith is by nature rather fluid, and it can, if we are not careful, simply flow from one thing or person to another thing or to someone else. Faith ebbs and flows along the way, and not so much from forces from the outside, although they do have an ongoing impact on our faith, but from forces within. But faith is always changing. All growth is change, even though all change is not growth. To grow, we must change. If we are not changing, then we are not growing. Since our faith in God is never absolute, nor is it ever completed in this life, and since it is never static, it must continue to grow, or it will begin to die.

We will wittingly or unwittingly choose which it is—either to see our faith in God wane, by default, through neglect or by otherwise living or thinking in ways that harm faith, or by our eager intent and actions.

Luke tells us the story of an incident that occurred in Jesus's last months on earth, when Christ gave his disciples a warnings and a command. The warning concerns causing others to

117

stumble. He says, "It would be better for them [the person caus-ing another to stumble] to be thrown into the sea with a mill-stone tied around their necks than to cause one of these little ones to stumble."[1] The second is a seemingly daunting command about the necessary extent of our forgiveness of one another: "Even if they sin against you seven times in a day and seven times come back to you saying, 'I repent,' you must forgive them."[2] Seven times in a day, huh? Really? Most of us have trouble truly forgiving another even once, especially when the pain or dam-age caused by such a sin is particularly acute.

And all they have to do to be forgiven is just to *say*, "I repent"? Hmm. What if they do not seem so sincere? What if their words and actions don't seem very contrite?

Continuing in the story, the apostles then, as if to say to them-selves, "Boy, have we got a long way to go," asked Jesus to "increase our faith."[3] These men had already been with him over two years. They had seen a powerful life doing incredible things—unbe-lievable things, in fact. And yet, they recognized, upon hearing such challenging, heart-level commands, that their faith would need to grow to obey such daunting dictates as these.

These guys had been with him on the boat in a horrible storm. They had seen him do what only God could do, and wondered as to he really was. Thinking they were about to drown with the sinking boat, Matthew tells us,

> The disciples went and woke him [Jesus], saying, "Lord, save us! We're going to drown!" He replied, "You of little faith, why are you so afraid?" Then he got up and rebuked the winds and the waves, and it was completely calm. The men were amazed and asked, "What kind of man is this? Even the winds and the waves obey him!"[4]

Well, of course they were afraid! What is difficult to under-stand about that? What normal human wouldn't be a bit afraid?

Rather than console them, though, and even before he took care of the storm, Jesus challenged them about how little their faith was. What were they supposed to believe? How were they to know—how am I to know—Jesus could and would calm the storm? What was it? Was their "little faith" evident in their failure to see that Jesus would remedy the situation? Or in their failure to recognize that he was actually God, and thus was in control of everything? Or was it in their fear of dying? Or was it just in their fear itself? The text doesn't spell that out for us; perhaps it was all of these. But after Jesus calmed the storm in front of their eyes. They were blown away, and they asked among themselves, "What kind of man is this? Even the winds and the waves obey him!" What kind of man is this? It's a question each of us must ask ourselves, perhaps over and over. And we need to answer it for ourselves over and over. For sure, the apostles had not yet caught on that they were dealing with God in the flesh. It is even harder for us to believe now.

So, of course, they needed their faith increased. Everyone does, in fact, because we all *live* by faith. We have to. There is no other choice. Whether we like it or not, we are constrained to live by faith in something or someone—be it people, things, academia, philosophy, places, idol gods, or God, however he be perceived by any one of us at any given time. Whether we are right about any of it or not.

Upon the apostles requesting that he increase their faith, Jesus uses the mustard seed metaphor saying, "If you have faith as small as a mustard seed, you can say to this mulberry tree, 'Be uprooted and planted in the sea,' and it will obey you."[5] Matthew tells us that on one occasion, Jesus said to them, "Truly I tell you, if you have faith as small as a mustard seed, you can say to this mountain, 'Move from here to there,' and it will move. Nothing will be impossible for you."[6] Whose faith, other than Jesus's, is big enough to order trees around, let alone to move mountains? Is Jesus being literal or only figurative in these statements? Either way, he is asserting that human faith is powerful indeed, especially when it is in the Almighty God!

Next, in Luke's account, Jesus uses a rather curious story about the responsibility of a servant to do what he was told to do and not to expect to be thanked by the master. The message for the apostles, as explained by Jesus, was, "So you also, when you have done everything you were told to do, should say, 'We are unworthy servants; we have only done our duty.'"[7] Okay then, they must have thought to themselves, Jesus is really pushing it, and this following him is going to take some serious faith and consideration. And perhaps they even thought themselves to be incapable of it.

Luke follows with the story of ten lepers who loudly beg Jesus to have pity on them. Whether their request for pity was actually for money, food, or healing is not told, but Jesus heals them, although his actual command was simply for them to "go show yourselves to the priests."[8] Luke tells us that "as they went, they were cleansed." Notice here the insistence on their acting out of faith—*as they went*, they were cleansed. Faith will never be inactive. Latent faith is no faith at all. Faith is active inwardly at first and outwardly as a result.

This story of the lepers reminds of another story of a blind man Jesus healed. He did it, oddly—at least to us today—by rubbing mud Jesus had made with his own saliva into the man's eyes and then sending him to wash in the Pool of Siloam.[9] As with the lepers, Jesus didn't simply heal the blind man on the spot. There was more to teach than the obvious. Rather, he told him to go and *do something*, and in trusting Jesus enough to do as he was told, he was healed.

It is no different with any of us today. Faith always calls for a decision on our part. And the right decision will call for action on our part as well.

This principle is also demonstrated in the Old Testament account of the visiting Syrian leader Naaman, who went to Israel after hearing of the powerful prophet Elisha. When he arrived, Elisha would not even come out to greet him and tersely sent someone else out to tell the visiting dignitary to just go dip in the Jordan seven times to be healed of his leprosy.[10] Naaman was insulted and angrily prepared to go back home. But there was obviously a deeper challenge command given here by the prophet. Medical practices current at the time had people doing all sorts of treatments, such as various kinds of dipping, using mudpacks, and such. So in actuality neither the blind man nor Naaman were being asked to do things particularly out of the ordinary. However, as anyone can attest, our willingness to follow such instructions from a doctor or healer will be in direct proportion to how much faith we have in them. In Naaman's case, an attendant prevailed upon him to give Elisha's command a try, at which he relented and did as the prophet asked. As the story tells us, after the seventh dip, he is said to have come up amazingly, completely healed!

With the lepers, their healing came as they went to present themselves to the priests, as commanded. With the blind man, his healing came as he washed in the Pool of Siloam, as commanded. With Naaman, his healing came after he dipped seven times in the Jordan, as commanded. Obedience is inextricably bound up in faith. Faith demands it, in fact. There can be "obedience" of sorts without faith; there can never be faith without obedience. The book of Hebrews essentially equates faith (belief) and obedience, noting, "And to whom did God swear that they would never enter his rest if not to those who disobeyed? So we see that they were not able to enter, because of their unbelief."[11]

Jesus commands us, as well, to *do* in order to *become*—to be healed, to receive his blessing, his presence, or whatever. He commissioned the apostles, saying, "Go make disciples…and I am with you always."[12] Paul commands, "Work out your salvation with fear and trembling, for it is God who works in you to will and to act in order to fulfill his good purpose."[13] In his Sermon on the Mount, Jesus says, "Seek first his kingdom and his righteousness, and all these things [life necessities] will be given to you as well."[14]

However, no one is to believe for one second that the power is in *our* doing. The clear intent in each of these cases was the power of God that was tapped into by the believing, the trusting, the having faith. And not just possessing some freestanding faith, but having faith in someone in particular. In these cases, they were called to have and to show faith in Jesus as the Christ.

Christ will be with us, work in us, and provide for us, just as with the apostles, the lepers, the blind man, and the leprous Naaman, *as we go.*

Believing is doing; doing is believing. Paul wrote,

For it is by grace you have been saved, through faith—and this is not from yourselves, it is the gift of God—not by works, so that no one can boast. For we are God's hand-iwork, created in Christ Jesus to do good works, which God prepared in advance for us to do.[15]

God's grace leads us to faith *in* him. Faith leads to effort and good, productive work *for* him. Or said differently, when we come to truly trust that God is in actuality who Jesus showed him to be, and not who and what Satan would have us believe him to be, our lives will reflect it in our diligence in our God-preappointed work, activities, and lives. In fact the "god" the dark side portrays to us, and tries to convince us is Yahweh, is, in fact, the arrogant, pride-ful, deceptive Satan himself. Jesus showed us who Yahweh really is—the Father God that is unbelievably humble, immeasurably graceful, infinitely loving, incredibly meek and lowly in heart, and so forth and so on. When we come to believe in the truth of the one true, living, loving, and graceful God, and he thus calls us back to himself, we are commissioned to do the good things that God has planned for us from the foundations of creation.

Ask the Lord to increase your faith, and then just do what faith leads you to do. Go!

Inspiration: The Old Testament story of Job has inspired countless people through the ages. It was written of Job, "This man was blameless and upright; he feared God and shunned evil."[16] This ancient writing is said by some to be one of the most lofty and well-written books ever. Clearly constructed in a poetic, dramatic fashion, it reads as a play, with Job and his friends the only actors. Job is portrayed as a righteous man and blessed with all the commensurate expectations most would have if they were as he. Then, all hell breaks loose—literally. God allows Satan to attack Job in order to show that not every human could be broken and made to lose faith in God. Everything is stripped from Job—his health, his wealth, and his family.[17] But it is written of Job that "in all this, Job did not sin by charging God with wrongdoing."[18]

The book tells the story of Job's grappling with the whys of his dilemma. And, no thanks to his misguided friends, he gets through it in an unbelievably faithful and persevering way. But not before God finally shows up and dresses him down royally for Job's naïve and ignorant insistence on knowing why God lets such bad stuff happen to us. However, through all he endured, Job did not curse God or give up his faith. In fact, he surely grew in his faith as hardship only intensified in his life. Even his questioning is an understandable expression of his belief that God had a good reason for allowing Job to suffer. Job just couldn't figure out why!

But in the end, as he promises each of us, God will rectify it all. God is just, which means God is fair. Job's story concludes noting, "The Lord blessed the latter part of Job's life more than the former part."[19] Job did not know why he had been dealt such misfortune. He hurt, he suffered, and he questioned, but he did not renounce trust in or curse God. In the end, he got better instead of bitter. He remained faithful, and God blessed him.

And God always keeps his promises! You can trust him; you can believe him; you can have a secure faith in him. Jesus said, "Be faithful, even to the point of death, and I will give you life as your victor's crown."[20] We must do what we are told by God to do in order to become who God wants us to be—returned to our original, unmarred condition as image bearers. Simply stated, our becoming like God is in our trusting him enough to do the things he tells us to do—go, wash, dip, share, serve, and so on. The doing is not what (who) empowers our actions or ultimately brings about good from all we do. God is working in us both to give us the will to do good and the power to carry it out, as well as extending to us the grace to cover over our incompetency, insufficiency, and sin that corrupts all we do in this fallen age.

For us, spiritual success is in our faith in the one who tells us what to think, what to believe, and what to do. Our doing or not doing it only testifies to the existence or nonexistence of faith in God. Our faith does this by, in some only-God-knows-how-and-why way, activating the only one who can truly do such things as moving mountains or telling trees what to do with simple but powerful statements such as, "'Let there be light,' and there was light,"[21] and so on.

Prayer: Lord, increase our faith. Help our trust in you to be ever maturing and increasing and flowing into many expressions of obedience to you.

Reflection: How has my faith increased over the course of my Christian walk? How does my faith need to increase? What can I do to help it to grow? What tends to stand in the way of my faith continually growing and increasing? What most causes my faith to wane?

References:
1. Luke 17:2.
2. Luke 17:4.
3. Luke 17:5.
4. Matt. 8:25–27.
5. Luke 17:6.
6. Matt. 17:20.
7. Luke 17:10.
8. Luke 17:14.
9. John 9:1–7.
10. 2 Kings 5:1–14.
11. Heb. 3:18–19.
12. Matt. 28:19–20.
13. Phil. 2:12–13.
14. Matt. 6:33.
15. Eph. 2:8–10.
16. Job 1:1.
17. Job 1:8–21.
18. Job 1:22.
19. Job 42:12.
20. Rev. 2:10.
21. Gen. 1:3.

20

My Lord and My God

Faith is not easy. Jesus, in fact, called it work.[1] In reality, mental, emotional, and spiritual effort can often seem more arduous than physical labor. Even though they be true, believing certain things can indeed be difficult. A reasoned out belief in the divine is most certainly one example. For instance, to deeply and honestly, with reasoned conviction, believe anything about the origins of the universe, be it in a divine creator or in some "natural" explanation, one will end up believing the seemingly unbelievable. And to actually turn a belief in an invisible but all-powerful being into a trust in him, to the point of giving our lives to him, is even more daunting to our human sensibilities.

The bigger questions that can be posed are many. Was the universe created? Who created it? Or how was it created? Why was it created? Or did it originate itself? If so, how? Is there a creator God we can know or might there be multiple gods, perhaps that we cannot know? Are there angels? And so forth. The proposed answers to these questions can multiply exponentially, even into the seemingly ridiculous. Francis Crick, noted British molecular biologist, humanist, and Christian antagonist, once proposed that the seeds of life my have been intentionally planted by extraterrestrials (a.k.a. directed panspermia).

Every conclusion reached will then elicit even more questions. For instance, if the universe was somehow self-originated in a big bang, then where did the original energy come from that produced this supposed burst of energy that transformed to matter? And if a God created it, where did that God come from? Is it more implausible to believe in an infinite God than it is to believe in infinite matter? Is it more implausible to believe God created it than it is to believe matter somehow self-created? Infinite existence in any form is simply outside the bounds of comprehension of our present finite reality of cause and effect.

Some physicists are now beginning to believe that human-kind will never know many things about the universe. And many Christians have come to believe that it is impossible to reconcile the Bible with many explanations and beliefs science proposes. But either way, believe some things we must, therefore, if we are to be wise, we should choose carefully our beliefs.

Scientists that accept the idea of a self-originated universe must study hard and reach deep to propose theories that are even mildly plausible. Critical-thinking theists must work just as hard to develop plausible ideas that reconcile what we read in the Bible with what is seen and observed scientifically. Many of us simply perpetuate the comfortable beliefs handed down to us and disregard a priori any other explanation, seemingly holding our hands over our ears, closing our eyes, and humming loudly to shut out all input. We've got our set story, and by golly, we're sticking with it!

When Jesus began his ministry, he came into a world that, although much more ancient than ours, was not really, at the core, all that different. There was turmoil and division among people. There were deeply divided opinions about politics, science, religion, and philosophy. There were political and religious wars. There existed, as today, plenty of prejudice, hate, and crime against others. There were an abundance of odd assumptions and conclusions about all the subjects that matter most. Israel had long expected the great king to come—the Messiah (Hebrew) or Christ (Greek)—who would finally liberate them and lead the nation to its own manifest destiny. Various individuals and groups had gone to great efforts to take control of God's chosen nation and just "make" God's promise happen. But, each ultimately failed miserably in its own time.

Our efforts to control—to play God—always fail miserably.

Even the concept of what the Messiah was to be was sorely misunderstood, distorted, and askew before and during Jesus's own time; it was based more on what the nation wanted—to be a powerful, conquering nation—than on biblical prophecy. And most assuredly, the concept of Messiah can be just as mentally and emotionally askew in our minds today. Perhaps some of Jesus's original disciples had already trained in the underground rebellion war tactics of their day in order to participate in a violent revolt against Roman control. Thus, Jesus's message of peace and an invisible kingdom did not sit well. Further, messianic prophecies never strongly indicated that the Messiah would manifest powers of healing, raising the dead and such. So both Jesus's behaviors and teachings caused confusion in the early disciples, not just because of his message, but because of their own human, preconceived, erroneous notions.

Our preconceived notions can often stand squarely in the way of an honest, objective search for truth. Sometimes our church upbringing can seemingly do more harm than good to our faith. We can become captives to a certain point of view and unable to think openly beyond it. Churches often seem more intent on indoctrinating members to their particular views, likely in order to maintain membership, than helping them to become lifelong seekers, learners, and effective thinkers. In other words, to make them true and eager disciples of the truth of Christ.

Jesus would be no less difficult for any one of us to believe in today, even if he were to walk with us again, than he was two thousand years ago, because truly believing in him requires thinking outside of the humanism box and daring to be different. Perhaps he's even harder to believe in now. Jesus once told a story of an unnamed rich man and a poor man named Lazarus who both died and went to a place he called Hades. The rich man was in torment and Lazarus was in comfort. The rich man was told that there was a gulf between the two sides of Hades that could not be crossed over. The rich man then asked Abraham to send Lazarus back to life to warn the rich man's five brothers about the place of torment he had gone to. Their exchange continues,

Abraham replied, "They have Moses and the prophets; let them listen to them." "No, father Abraham," he said, "but if someone from the dead goes to them, they will repent." He said to him, "If they do not listen to Moses and the prophets, they will not be convinced even if someone rises from the dead."[2]

Concerning the rich man's brothers, as with all of us who are still living, it is as if Abrham said, "People with their minds closed, will listen to nothing that contradicts their own beliefs, no matter where it comes from." We've already decided on a thing. We've moved on. It is amazing how unbelieving humanity can be, even in the face of obvious evidence. Distrust seems intrinsic to our survival instincts. But, as Abraham notes, resurrection or no resurrection, they will only accept what they already want to believe, even though they already have the law and the prophets, which point them directly to Jesus as the Messiah. The point of view of the rich man's living brothers would have been, as it often is with far too many of us who are still living, as was said centuries ago by the Greek orator, Demosthenes, "We believe whatever we want to believe."

Exactly—if we won't listen to the evidence, we won't listen to any other reasoning, no matter how compelling, for instance, a resurrection from the dead might be. What should it take for anyone to believe in a creator God? What evidence would ever be enough?

This faith dilemma is really quite understandable though. Faith is hard, especially faith that will cost us something. Changing our actual underlying belief tenets can be even harder. Change in belief dictates change in lifestyle. We get comfortable in our present lifestyles and social groups, and we mostly don't want to change. Most believers do not like to admit faith is hard. Neither do many scientists, philosophers, and humanists like to admit they live by faith as well, and that their faith is equally hard, and arguably even harder, to maintain.

The apostle Thomas is sometimes called "doubting Thomas" because of a postresurrection encounter and exchange he had with Jesus.[3] In his account of the resurrection, the apostle John records that Mary Magdalene was the first to discover the empty tomb. All four of the gospel writers record the last encounters in different ways. All of the accounts were finally written down, likely more than three decades later, and demonstrate the unique and amazing way the revelation was inspired through multiple perspectives.[4] Their disparity can bewilder; their agreement can astound. Luke tells us that Jesus appeared to various individuals and groups of disciples over a forty-day period to give them "convincing proofs" that he was alive and to give them instructions about the emerging kingdom of God.[5]

Does Thomas really stand out as any different from any thoughtful human being when none of the apostles really understood from the things Jesus said that he would actually rise in bodily form from the dead? Can doubt not be evidence that belief exists? The reality is that all the disciples were all pretty shocked by Jesus's literal resurrection, not just from death, but from such a torturous death! John tells us that after Mary Magdalene told Peter and him about the empty tomb, the two of them ran there. Although he arrived ahead of Peter, John writes,

> Then, Simon Peter came along behind him and went straight into the tomb. He saw the strips of linen lying there, as well as the cloth that had been wrapped around Jesus's head. The cloth was still lying in its place, separate from the linen. Finally, the other disciple, who had reached the tomb first, also went inside. He saw and believed.[6]

John explained that it was only after he personally saw the empty tomb that he believed fully. He adds an explanatory note, however, to the experience, saying, "They still did not understand from scripture that Jesus had to rise from the dead."[7] Up to that point, none of them had understood, even though Jesus had told them, as the apostle Matthew records,

> From that time on, Jesus began to explain to his disciples that he must go to Jerusalem and suffer many things at

the hands of the elders, the chief priests, and the teachers of the law, and that he must be killed and on the third day be raised to life.[8]

None of them were getting it because it was confusing from the human perspective, and because they didn't get what was to happen, they didn't believe it when it did happen. Jesus had, after all, been teaching them, trying to express and explain truths of the invisible kingdom of God in parables, idioms, metaphors, symbolism, and other ways that often seemed unfamiliar to them. Hence their inability to grasp the concrete meanings is certainly understandable.

So Thomas simply represents by proxy all of us in a way. John describes Thomas's encounter with the risen Lord this way:

Now Thomas (also known as Didymus, one of the Twelve) was not with the disciples when Jesus came. So the other disciples told him, "We have seen the Lord!" But he said to them, "Unless I see the nail marks in his hands and put my finger where the nails were and put my hand into his side, I will not believe." A week later, his disciples were in the house again, and Thomas was with them. Though the doors were locked, Jesus came and stood among them and said, "Peace be with you!" Then he said to Thomas, "Put your finger here; see my hands. Reach out your hand and put it into my side. Stop doubting and believe." Thomas said to him, "My Lord and my God!"[9]

Thomas speaks for all of us concerning when we finally *get it*, when we finally see the risen Lord: "My Lord and my God!" Yes, generally speaking, today we must encounter Jesus through the testimony of those who gave their lives up to testify to what he did and who he was. But then we can encounter him through our own personal experiences.[10] And we can only accept in our hearts that it is Christ we are encountering when we have become convinced of the reasons to believe. Then, we can confidently accept the foundational salvation principle, as Paul wrote:

> If you declare with your mouth, "Jesus is Lord," and believe in your heart that God raised him from the dead, you will be saved. For it is with your heart that you believe and are justified, and it is with your mouth that you profess your faith and are saved.[11]

Real faith can only be said to exist when a logical acceptance of the reality that Jesus Christ was indeed raised from the dead (believing with the mind) is internalized (believing with the heart) and is by necessity professed with the mouth (expressing in life). Paul reminded the Corinthians of just this when, in his letter to them, he reviewed that they had received the gospel (logically accepted it as truth in their minds), taken a stand for the gospel (surrendered to it in their hearts, where behavior is controlled), and were holding to the gospel without turning back (professing with their life, for the "righteous will live by faith").[12]

For each individual today who encounters Christ and accepts him by faith as both Lord and Savior comes the blessing Jesus told Thomas about: "Because you have seen me, you have believed; blessed are those who have not seen and yet have believed."[13]

It is often said that, "seeing is believing." A truism, it is supposed. A necessity, it is most certainly not! Many, and arguably most, of the beliefs inherent to civilization are based on that which cannot be seen with our human eyes or personally witnessed. And ultimately the greatest blessings are found in these. Jesus pronounced just such blessing on those in the succeeding generations to follow him, who would not be able to witness his unbelievable life, but who would believe because of the testimony of those that did!

If you see him, really get the reality of the resurrected Christ, your response too will surely be "My Lord and My God!"

Inspiration: Art prodigy Akiane Kramarik was born to atheist parents in a secluded and quite modest existence in Illinois.

Stating she was born in a shack, she describes her early life this way: "Our family had no money, no friends, no relatives, no television or radio. Our life was quite simple—long walks in nature, open conversations, and hands-on explorations of knowledge."[14] In her early life, there was no religion, no prayer, and no discussions of God or religion, including Christianity. Though insulated from information about God or Christ, she began to describe visions she was experiencing of both. She began to paint at four years of age, and at eight, she painted the face of Jesus in a work she called *Prince of Peace*. She went on to create nine more such paintings of Christ. Her parents were befuddled.

Later, a young man named Colton Burpo had his own heavenly experiences as described by his father in the book *Heaven Is for Real*.[15] His father showed him many supposed and traditional pictures of Jesus, each of which Colton rejected as not looking like the Jesus he had seen in heaven—at least until his father, without any pre-qualification, showed him Akiane's *Prince of Peace* portrait. When Colton saw the painting (again, without foreknowledge of what he was being shown), he is said to have instantly identified it as being the Jesus he saw in his own heavenly vision.

Two young people, two separate visions, same picture. Yes, faith is hard because doubt and suspicion are strong in us. We would rather doubt than believe because we fear being taken advantage of or being made a fool of, both of which are possible. But God is alive and well. The creation emanates from him, not the other way around. In his own testimony, Paul said that when everyone deserted him, Christ stood by his side.[16] The resurrected Jesus Christ was indeed an existential reality to the apostle Paul.

The spiritual realms intersect our physical realm and interact with it, as even scripture attests. The book of Hebrews says some have entertained angels when they were unaware of it.[17] The Bible contains quite a few accounts of these intersects between our visible world and the invisible one. Thus, our faith begins with knowledge, is internalized to become conviction, is expressed in profession of life and lips, and can be gloriously experienced through constant awareness of the divine in our midst, from which our very substance and being emanates.

Prayer: Lord, meet us where our weak and faltering faith fails us as we reach out to you. May we experience you in a way that causes us to declare in awe, "My Lord and my God!" Flowing from our reasoned conviction, may our hearts strain, by faith, to reach out to you in the spiritual realms.

Reflection: What is the substance of my own faith? What is the substance of my doubts? Where is it and how is it that I may have experienced Christ, wittingly or unwittingly? How can I be more spiritually quickened and be more alert and aware of my interactions with the invisible spiritual world?

References:

1. John 6:29.
2. Luke 16:29–31.
3. John 20:24–28.
4. Matt. 28:1–20; Mark 16:1–20; Luke 24:1–53; John 20:1–30; Acts 1:1–11; 1 Cor. 15:1–11.
5. Acts 1:3.
6. John 20:6–8.
7. John 20:9.
8. Matt. 16:21.
9. John 20:24–28.
10. John 14:23; Acts 2:38–39.
11. Rom. 10:9–10.
12. 1 Cor. 15:1–2.
13. John 20:29.
14. Mark Ellis, *For Child Art Prodigy Akiane, Jesus is for Real,* United Stares: Godreports, http://blog.godreports.com/2012/01/for-child-art-prodigy-akiane-jesus-is-for-real/, January 4, 2012.
15. Todd Burpo, *Heaven is for Real,* Nashville: Nelson Books, 2010.
16. 2 Tim. 4:16.
17. Heb. 13:2.

21

Indecision Is Often the Worst Decision of All

Adam and Eve had probably, for some time before actually doing so, wavered in their commitment to not touch or eat fruit from the Tree of the Knowledge of Good and Evil.[1] Such indecision flows from the lack of conviction.

After the flood and during the time leading up to the Tower of Babel, the people had surely been wavering about obeying God, putting off making a decision about spreading out and rein-habiting the earth—that is, before actually and finally deciding not to.[2] Indecision often precedes bad decisions! Oh, they tried to justify their disobedience with their notable sham to build a "tower to heaven," perhaps that would distract God from dealing with their disobedience in refusing to disburse, as he'd commanded them. They preferred to put most of their effort into making a name for themselves. In building the tower, they broke faith with God and were likely trying to placate him, rather than trust and obey him. God is not to be placated by human subterfuge. Everything he commands us has an exact purpose.

The fruit of the bad tree has continued to devastate humanity right up to today. Humanism, defined here as trusting in and depending on ourselves rather than believing in and depending on God, has continued, from the first bad decision made by Eve and Adam, to wreak destruction on emerging humanity. And in their indecision—their refusal to firmly decide to obey God—they had already been disobedient anyway. Indecision was their decision. Such indecision is the inner erosion of human character. It is double-mindedness. Simply not obeying is just as bad as disobeying. It is merely an expression of disobedience. God is recorded in scripture as often quick to punish inactivity and complacency concerning his expressed will.[3]

It was Moses who was later charged with leading Israel out of Egypt and to the land God had promised them—Canaan's land. It was a frustrating, difficult two-year trek. Because of their disobedience, it turned into a tormenting forty-year wilderness wandering. During this time, God, in effect, raised up a new generation of Israelites. He did it by allowing everyone over twenty years of age to die during the forty years in the wilderness, that is, except for Moses, Joshua, and Caleb, who were allowed to survive to lead the nation. God would ultimately take Moses and quietly bury him before their final entry into Canaan.[4] However, before his death, as he prepared them for the conquest, Moses challenged the people of God to be decisive, saying,

> This day I call the heavens and the earth as witnesses against you that I have set before you life and death, blessings and curses. Now choose life, so that you and your children may live and that you may love the Lord your God, listen to his voice, and hold fast to him. For the Lord is your life, and he will give you many years in the land he swore to give to your fathers, Abraham, Isaac, and Jacob.[5]

Make the decision. Make the firm call. Decide!

Choose life. Just choose. Make a decision to live—a real, hard, firm decision. Choosing God is always the right decision. Choosing God means to do what he says. Indecision concerning making the choice for God is its own decision—and it is always a wrong choice! God wants us to operate in the now, not in perpetual postponement.[6] Making the right decisions today secures the best results tomorrow. Many of today's problems can easily be traced to indecisiveness in times passed.

Israel's new leader, Joshua, again called the children of Israel to a decision for God, saying, "If serving the Lord seems undesirable to you, then choose for yourselves this day whom you will serve."[7] It is as if he is saying, "Just finally choose, for crying out loud! Your indecision is killing you!"

Their decision-making always wavered between good and bad, right and wrong, though, and hundreds of years later, Elijah was again challenging Israel's idolatrous descendants, who were still waffling, saying to them, "How long will you waver between two opinions? If the Lord is God, follow him; but if Baal is God, follow him."[8] Stop your cowardice and indecision—make a call. Decide.

God hates indecision and the endemic apathy and complacency that pervades those who lack conviction. In his prophecy against Judah, the southern kingdom during the times of the divided kingdom, Zephaniah speaks for God, saying, "At that time, I will search Jerusalem with lamps and punish those who are complacent."[9] God is indeed angered by complacency and will punish those who are complacent. The prophet Zephaniah lived and led during the time of Josiah, the reformer king of Judah. Josiah was one of the few actual good guys among the kings of both Judah and Israel. However, even under Josiah's righteous leadership and his attempts at faithful reform, the rank and file remained complacent, stuck in the middle with no conviction, no strong decision—not too unlike the church membership at large today. Indecisiveness is endemic to poor, shortsighted leadership and churches.

Decisions—especially the big ones—can be difficult for all of us. But indecision can be more difficult, and arguably the worst decision of all, even though, in the short run, it may feel easier.

Jesus once challenged a young man to make a firm decision to follow him.[10] This was an apparently nice guy who'd come to ask the "good teacher" what he had to do to inherit eternal life. Jesus told him to obey the law, mentioning only the last six commandments involving the treatment of other people, saying "You shall not murder, you shall not commit adultery, you shall not steal, you shall not give false testimony, you shall not defraud, honor your father and mother." Most assuredly, Jesus, intentionally, did not mention the first four commandments involving our devotion to God. The young man excitedly told him he had done those six things his whole life. But there were four commands that preceded the six Jesus mentioned. The unmentioned ones were about God: you shall have no other gods before me, you shall have no idols you worship, you shall not misuse God's name in vain or in useless ways, and you shall keep the Sabbath as holy (set apart) for God. Those must have cut to the quick of the young man.[11]

Mark finishes the story, "Jesus looked at him and loved him. 'One thing you lack,' he said. 'Go, sell everything you have and give to the poor, and you will have treasure in heaven. Then come, follow me.' At this, the man's face fell. He went away sad because he had great wealth."[12] He may have decided in that moment not to follow Jesus, because he wasn't willing to pay the price. Likely, he thought he would just put off making the decision. People, and young people especially, often do that concerning Christ. Perhaps the man changed his mind later and came back. Some might argue that the young man decided at that time not to follow Jesus. However, it also can be argued that it was mere indecision that kept him away. He obviously believed Jesus was a good teacher or he wouldn't have come asking him such a questions. Jesus's Messiahship was not questioned in the story. But, the "good" guy was apparently tripped up in his commitment to God. Subsequently, his indecision in that moment was arguably the worst decision of all!

The ditches and gutters of history are littered with those who fell by the wayside in indecision. Missed opportunities. Decisions made too late. Failures to act in critical moments. True indecision is the result of weak faith. It is a lack of conviction exposing itself in a lack of zeal and devotion. A line, sometimes fine and at other times broad, exists between wise and essential deliberation before making an important decision about an issue and blatant indecision. The situation and the decision itself will determine which it is. Godly wisdom demands us to determine even that.

But following Jesus requires bold, decisive action, often on a moment's notice. Thus, our hearts and minds must be trained, in advance, for the challenges to come.

Jesus was not indecisive, however. He demonstrated his passion over and over: "Zeal for your house will consume me."[13] And Paul commanded us not to be that way either: "Never be lacking in zeal, but keep your spiritual fervor, serving the Lord."[14] Serving the Lord faithfully requires zeal. And zeal is the result of the kind of faith that grows from a deep conviction about the truth and the reality that "Jesus is Lord."

In his messages to the seven churches of Asia, in the book of Revelation, Jesus delivered a particularly challenging admonition to the Laodicea church, saying, "I know your deeds, that you are neither cold nor hot. I wish you were either one or the other! So, because you are lukewarm—neither hot nor cold— I am about to spit you out of my mouth."[15] Middle-of-the-road complacency, indecisiveness, and lukewarmness clearly make God sick or even angry. He's not going to put up with it long. God has little patience with indecision in light of specific calls to faith, devotion, and action.

The church in Laodicea foreshadows the good, nice church of today, whose members might be called the nice, together, "cool" Christians—urbane, acculturated in the world, strong, independent, of sufficient means, and perhaps impressive to the world. It is the kind of church that the world generally approves of and even likes, the church that doesn't offend the sensibilities of the complacent. It is the one that is committed but not *too* committed. But Jesus sees it a completely different way: "You say, 'I am rich; I have acquired wealth and do not need a thing.' But you do not realize that you are wretched, pitiful, poor, blind, and naked."[16] Jesus assesses their inward reality in quite a contrast to how they might have appeared outwardly. They appeared successful, prosperous, and confident, but only on the outside, not on the inside. Inside they were morally destitute and shameful. Appearances can deceive. And often they do. Too many of us are prone to look at ourselves only on the outside through the mirrors of the world, rather than seeing ourselves through the eyes of Christ.[17]

Jesus thus called the lot of the Laodacean church to collectively repent, literally to change their minds: "Those whom I love I rebuke and discipline. So be earnest and repent. Here I am! I stand at the door and knock. If anyone hears my voice and opens the door, I will come in and eat with that person, and they with me."[18] The lukewarm Christian and the lukewarm church—the complacent, cool ones—have closed hearts. They become tepid, still, useless pools—murky, stagnant ponds lacking clarity. They are fruitless, or worse yet bear bad fruit, and they grow increasingly toxic within themselves and to others. Such Christians and their churches are as seemingly lovely fruit trees with stately shapes and rich, beautiful greenery, but that are barren of good fruit and are purposeless, beyond serving as impressive decorations. The heart that is closed off from Christ is a dark and dying heart, because it is a heart that is being separated from Christ.[19] Sin breeds and increases in such darkness through deception and hidden means. It is never hidden from God though, and he is never deceived about it. He sees us in our deepest inner places.[20] We can fool ourselves; we can fool others; but, we cannot fool God! In such a scenario, we only show ourselves to be fools.

Christ does not want to be *a* lord in our life; he will only be *the* Lord of all of our life everyday of the week.[21] It is nonnegotiable. Jesus is not just to be for us *a* way among some imaginary pluralistic mirage; he is to be *the* one and only way. He is not just *a* truth; he is *the* truth. And he is not just *a* life path; he is *the* life.[22]

Christ has called each of us to be his ambassadors, to be citizens of and represent another country. He calls us to be aliens in this world and to call others into another kingdom: "The kingdom of God has come near. Repent and believe the good news!"[23] We are to call the world to an eternal decision. And our ambassadorship flows from our conviction about his eternal kingdom and his love for humankind—the love that ought to compel us to decide to live our lives for him.[24] Thus, Paul explains,

So from now on, we regard no one from a worldly point of view. Though we once regarded Christ in this way, we do so no longer. Therefore, if anyone is in Christ, the new creation has come: the old has gone, the new is here! All this is from God, who reconciled us to himself through Christ and gave us the ministry of reconciliation: that God was reconciling the world to himself in Christ, not counting people's sins against them. And he has committed to us the message of reconciliation. We are, therefore, Christ's ambassadors, as though God were making his appeal through us. We implore you on Christ's behalf: be reconciled to God. God made him who had no sin to be sin for us, so that in him, we might become the righteousness of God.[25]

Paul continues, saying that it is decision time: "I tell you, now is the time of God's favor, now is the day of salvation."[26]

Every day is decision time. Now is the day of salvation. Now is the day to decide what we believe. Now is the day to choose whom we will serve. Now is the day to take up our own cross and follow him. Following or not following Christ is always the decision of decisions. Whether or not we do so deliberately, we make the choice concerning following him—to do so or not to do so—every day we live. Indeed we make the decision in every moment we live! We lay it all on the line eternally by what we choose. And we are assured we will ultimately live with our choice. Is he Lord, or is he not Lord?

The odds are in favor of Jesus Christ being the Lord of lords and the King of kings. The creation declares it. The historical record confirms it. The scriptures proclaim it. However, each of us must make our own personal decision, and then we must live respective to our decision.

Inspiration: Famous civil rights and national leader, Martin Luther King Jr., once said, "The time is always right to do right." It was he, more than anyone else, who called America to finally materialize the dream of our forefathers to be a nation where, in reality and practice, "all men are created equal." King said, "Faith is taking the first step even when you don't see the whole staircase." About indecisiveness and inaction, he once said, "In the end, we will remember not the words of our enemies but the silence of our friends"—their silence brought on by fear, by their lack of faith and conviction, their indecision. He also said, "The ultimate measure of a man is not where he stands in moments of comfort and convenience, but where he stands at times of challenge and controversy." In another speech, he said, "The ultimate tragedy is not the oppression and cruelty by the bad people but the silence over that by the good people." James writes, " If anyone, then, knows the good they ought to do and doesn't do it, it is sin for them."[27]

The silence of the good people is indeed the ultimate tragedy. Eighteenth-century British statesman Edmund Burke said, "The only thing necessary for the triumph of evil is for good men to do nothing." Martin Luther King Jr. dared to do something, and it cost him his life, just as Jesus, the ultimate example, dared to do something and gave his life for it. Indecision, along with its fruit of doing nothing, is generally the hedge of the lazy, the cowardly, and those lacking conviction. In a 1910 speech in France, Theodore Roosevelt spoke these timeless and challenging words, especially for those frozen by indecision:

It is not the critic who counts, not the man who points out how the strong man stumbles or where the doer of deeds could have done them better. The credit belongs to the man who is actually in the arena, whose face is marred by dust and sweat and blood, who strives valiantly, who errs, who comes short again and again, because there is no effort without error and shortcoming; but who does actually strive to do the deeds; who knows great enthusiasms, the great devotions; who spends himself in a worthy cause; who at the best knows in the end the triumph of high achievement, and who at the worst, if he fails, at least fails while daring greatly, so that his place shall never be

with those cold and timid souls who neither know victory
nor defeat.[28]

Short of foolishness, it is always better to do something wrong
when trying to do what is right than to make the ultimate mistake
of never attempting anything that is worthy of a life lived well.
A famous but painfully true misquotation all-too-well describes
the masses of humanity in this way: "Most men lead lives of quiet
desperation and go to the grave with the song still in them."[29]

The apostle Paul was a man of great conviction and is arguably the most influential man in history next to Jesus Christ himself. Near the end of his life, he described his own life conviction
this way: "I know whom I have believed and am convinced that
he is able to guard what I have entrusted to him until that day."[30]
When Paul came to believe, he laid it all on the line. He was *all
in* always. What do we believe and how strongly do we believe
it? Paul believed so strongly that he used the word "know" to
describe his conviction.

Our decision is perhaps best seen in the words of an inspiring
Christian song, "I have decided to follow Jesus, no turning back,
no turning back." These are especially inspiring words, because
they are derived from a story passed on telling of a nineteenth-
century man from India who spoke them when being threatened by the village chief with the death of himself and his family
if he did not renounce his faith in Christ. He did not renounce
his faith, but rather spoke the words in the song lyrics. His wife,
his sons, and he were executed. However, it is reported that his
conviction and decisiveness in the face of execution led to the
conversion of the village chief and other villagers.[31] His decision echoed the decision of the Lord Jesus Christ himself when
he chose to come and to die for us. The apostle Paul writes an
admonition to us concerning following Christ's example, saying,

> In your relationships with one another, have the same
> mind-set as Christ Jesus, who, being in very nature God,
> did not consider equality with God something to be used

to his own advantage; rather, he made himself nothing by taking the very nature of a servant, being made in human likeness. And being found in appearance as a man, he humbled himself by becoming obedient to death—even death on a cross![32]

The time is always right to do right. So, decide. And, do it now.

Prayer: Father, help me to be a person of faith and conviction, that I may be a person of decision. Free me from the grip of fearful indecision, and deliver me into the hands of faithful choices. May I be among those who act in the face of need and who dare to speak up when other voices are silent. May I, in the spirit of the apostle Paul, be able to confidently say, "I believed; therefore I have spoken."[33]

Reflection: Have I truly decided to follow Jesus, not just say I do? Does this decision lead me into powerful and self-sacrificing decisions in serving him? If so, how? Or do I live in lukewarm complacency and apathy? Why or why not?

References:
1. Gen. 3:1–7.
2. Gen. 11:1–9.
3. Zeph. 1:12; 1 Sam. 15:1-25.
4. Deut. 34:5-6.
5. Deut. 30:19–20.
6. Matt. 6:33-34; Zeph. 1:12; Luke 9:23; 2 Cor. 6:1; Heb. 3:13; Rev. 3:20
7. Josh. 24:15.
8. 1 Kings 18:21.
9. Zeph. 1:12.
10. Mark 10:17-22.
11. Ex. 20:1-17.
12. Mark 10:21–22.
13. John 2:17; Psa. 69:9.
14. Rom. 12:11.

15. Rev. 3:15–16.
16. Rev. 3:17.
17. 2 Cor. 5:16-17.
18. Rev. 3:19–20.
19. John 15:6-8.
20. Heb. 4:12-13.
21. Luke 9:23.
22. John 14:6.
23. Mark 1:15.
24. 2 Cor. 5:12–15.
25. 2 Cor. 5:16–21.
26. 2 Cor. 6:2.
27. James 4:17.
28. Excerpt from the speech "Citizenship In A Republic" delivered at the Sorbonne, in Paris, France on April 23, 1910.
29. The first half of the quote was likely from Henry David Thoreau's *Walden*; the second half from Oliver Wendell Holmes's *The Voiceless*: "Alas for those that never sing, But die with all their music in them."
30. 2 Tim. 1:12.
31. Information taken from the online magazine, "God-Fashioned," September 16, 2016, http://www.godfashioned.com/songsept10.
32. Phil. 2:5–8.
33. 2 Cor. 4:13; Psa. 116:10.

22

Tenacity of Faith Is Born of Adversity in Life

Seek not to avoid all adversity; seek not to merely survive adversity; seek rather to thrive in adversity, for that must be our brave and honest quest. James said, "Consider it pure joy, my brothers and sisters, whenever you face trials of many kinds, because you know that the testing of your faith produces perseverance."[1] Hebrews admonishes us to, "Endure hardship as discipline."[2]

Hardship is not a bad thing; rather, it is an essential thing to the one who would grow in faith. For the disciple, it is to be an expected thing, a promised thing—as Jesus said, "I have told you these things, so that in me you may have peace. In this world, you will have trouble. But take heart! I have overcome the world."[3] And as the apostle Paul wrote, "In fact, everyone who wants to live a godly life in Christ Jesus will be persecuted."[4]

Perhaps it might be expressed best poetically in this way,

Oh, the bliss of peaceful serving,
Delight, enjoyment, in our hands,
Bitterness when life betrays us,
Life our happy hope remands.

Many are the persons who rejoice in serving God when all is well but become bitter and stop in times of trouble. Too many are the false prophets who would promise only happiness and prosperity to those deemed most faithful, suggesting, therefore, that the lack of outward blessings must somehow signal a lack of faithfulness. One can make money most easily from those who are fearful or who feel guilty. Thus, "Do not listen to what the prophets are prophesying to you; they fill you with false hopes."[5] Yes, false prophets will indeed fill you false hopes as well as try to provoke emotions within you to motivate you toward their schemes of personal gain and fame.

Adversity, while not to be intentionally sought out, is the friend of the one who would increase their faith and grow nearer to God. God, as our loving Father, will sometimes bring adversity to us. "For it is better, if it is God's will, to suffer for doing good than for doing evil."[6] Suffering will come to us all, many times not first because of outside influences but often due to our own or others' sins and mistakes. But suffering also will come to us for our doing good, and it is for benefit. All adversity can turn out for our benefit if we endure it according to God's instructions. God, in fact, works out everything for good, for those called by him and who love him.[7]

But in the end, rather than leading to only pain and destruction, suffering can bring maturation, strength, and tenacity of spirit: "And the God of all grace, who called you to his eternal glory in Christ, after you have suffered a little while, will himself restore you and make you strong, firm, and steadfast."[8] Thus, "It is good for a man to bear the yoke while he is young."[9]

The world would convince us that pain is bad and pleasure is good, that God is good if he brings us pleasure and prosperity but bad if he allows us or others to suffer. And sometimes pain can, indeed, come from bad, and certainly many pleasures are blessings from God that are meant to be enjoyed. But Christ reminds us that sometimes it is pain that is good, and that many of the pleasures we seek out to mitigate our hurt can be harmful. It is good "to bear the yoke" as we grow up. Such a yoke of challenge, of pain, and even of suffering, whether it be brought on us by God or just permitted by the Lord, is intended to work out for our good, and its results will be far greater than what we would have had otherwise. Comfort, pleasure, and ease yield little good in those whose faith is weak and see their Christian walk as one of self-indulgence. These will only be thankful when all seems well but are resentful and angry when circumstances are otherwise. God wants us to be thankful in *all* circumstances, whether they bring happiness or hurt to us.[10]

As we grasp the gospel of Christ, our faith in the immeasurable grace of God frees us from mere animal survival and allows us to live above and beyond the present realm, into the heavenly realms.[11] The apostle Paul writes of the hope we have in Christ that allows us to view pain and difficulty the opposite of how the world sees it. He writes,

> Therefore, since we have been justified through faith, we have peace with God through our Lord Jesus Christ, through whom we have gained access by faith into this grace in which we now stand. And we boast in the hope of the glory of God. Not only so, but we also glory in our sufferings, because we know that suffering produces perseverance; perseverance, character; and character, hope. And hope does not put us to shame because God's love has been poured out into our hearts through the Holy Spirit, who has been given to us.[12]

Following Paul's line of thought, we see that God justifies us through our faith in him; that is, we come to be on peaceful terms with God through Jesus Christ. We become straight up with God. Because of our faith in God, we are given access to his grace offered to all humanity through Christ Jesus our Lord. Thus our boast and our hope lie in God's glory—his power and goodness—not in our own ability to control our lives and destinies or to be good within ourselves in any way independent of his empowering grace.

And thus armed with this reality, we are able to rejoice and see glory in our sufferings in this present life, because we know that, through Christ, suffering produces perseverance, which produces character, which produces hope. And this hope—this very real expectation that is not just a wish—will not cause us shame in the end, but rather, it will bring us glory. It is through this hope he gives us that God has expressed his love to us and poured it into our hearts through the blessed Holy Spirit that he has given to us through Christ.

So a measure of pain and suffering is our present reality, and yes, our need, as we live in Christ. Our enemy, the devil, knows our good, eternal fate is sealed by God and that his own bad destiny is fixed and beyond his control. Peter thus offers an important caution and admonition concerning the evil one, saying,

> Be alert and of sober mind. Your enemy the devil prowls around like a roaring lion looking for someone to devour. Resist him, standing firm in the faith, because you know that the family of believers throughout the world is undergoing the same kind of sufferings.[13]

As God's chosen people, we indeed must be on our guard against the devil's schemes against us: "For we are not unaware of his schemes."[14] We must not be naïve and unbelieving. We must resist, rather than succumb, to him. We must not cower in the face of the pain and suffering he brings upon us in this present time. We are not alone. We have never been alone. We will never be alone. God is never far from any one of us.[15]

And we can rest assured that "the Lord is close to the brokenhearted and saves those who are crushed in spirit."[16] So we can confidently echo the words of the apostle Paul,

> We are hard pressed on every side but not crushed; perplexed but not in despair; persecuted but not abandoned; struck down but not destroyed. We always carry around in our body the death of Jesus, so that the life of Jesus may also be revealed in our body.[17]

So, in the face of pain and suffering, be tenacious, be bold, be confident, and endure pain as a brave soldier. Your faith will grow because of it and, most assuredly, good will come from it.

Inspiration: In Genesis 37–47, the story of Joseph is told, and it stands as an ageless story of grace and faith in the midst of pain and trial. Joseph couldn't help that he was his father's favorite, and he couldn't help that his brothers were jealous of him. It was not by his own choice that God gave him two visions of his brothers bowing down to him (something he could, however, have kept to himself). Joseph was not perfect; but, he was faithful. In an ancient, barbaric world, his own brothers first threatened to kill him but then sold him to slave traders heading to Egypt. They told his father, Jacob, that Joseph had been killed. They dipped Joseph's special coat, given to him by his father, in goat's blood and presented it to Jacob to convince him Joseph had been killed by wild animals. Joseph was sold as a slave into the home of the well-to-do captain of the guard, Potiphar. But Joseph worked hard there, directing the affairs of the wealthy, powerful man. He was faithful and was given leadership over all the household and fields, where he would learn about Egyptian culture and agriculture.

However, Potiphar's wife attempted to seduce him and, after having been rejected by Joseph, told her husband that Joseph had tried to rape her. Joseph was thrown into Pharaoh's dungeon, where he surely learned Egyptian politics and especially about Pharaoh, the king of Egypt, himself. After some time there, by an act of God, he was able to interpret the dreams of two of Pharaoh's servants who had also been thrown into the dungeon. The dreams foretold the death of one and the return to palace services of the other. When Pharaoh himself had a vision from God, the servant finally remembered Joseph, who was called in to interpret the dream. The dream was that there would be abundance in the land for seven years to be followed by seven years of intense drought and famine.

Upon seeing Joseph's ability to interpret his dream—and likely learning more about his leadership skills that had been made evident in Potiphar's house and in the dungeon—Pharaoh made Joseph overlord of Egypt, under only the king himself. Joseph was to be in charge of preparing and managing all of Egypt during the years of bounty and then through the years of famine. In all of this injustice and pain, Joseph was faithful, and God allowed him to excel. By God's divine will and guidance, Joseph successfully navigated Egypt through the preparations for the famine and then through the throes of it. Next, his brothers, still living with their father as foreigners in the Promised Land, were sent by Jacob to Egypt to get food. The famine had proven just as severe in the Land of Canaan as it was in Egypt. Thus, the brothers had to go before Joseph, whom they'd treated treacherously, and bow down to him, as foretold in Joseph's original vision. They were still unaware of Joseph's identity however when they came to purchase food.

Joseph eventually identified himself to them, to their great shock and terror. Joseph reflected aloud on the reality of the faithful person he'd become in the midst of the injustice done against him and the suffering his brothers' actions had brought on him. He summarized it all, saying, "And now, do not be distressed and do not be angry with yourselves for selling me here, because it was to save lives that God sent me ahead of you...it was not you who sent me here but God. He made me father to the pharaoh, lord of his entire household and ruler of all Egypt"[18] Joseph was faithful to God through all of the injustice and hardship he suffered. And as people of God, we too must always trust that "it is God who works in you [us] to will and to act in order to fulfill his good purpose."[19] Therefore, we can be brave and hopeful in the face of our pain and suffering, just as Joseph was through his own.

Prayer: Lord, help me to become better, not bitter, when faced with trial and suffering. Build my faith deeply in the reality of Jesus as Lord and grow from it a rock-solid hope within me. May I be one on whom you can depend. May I be as Joseph in my trust for you. May I be one, as Job, who can, if called upon, serve in suffering, as a testimony to your incomparable power, ultimate goodness, and absolute faithfulness. May my faith produce within me an unquestioned tenacity for Christ, who is to be praised forever and ever!

Reflection: How tenacious is my faith? What pain and suffering have I endured, and how have I held up under it? How can I grow my faith in Christ that I may be a faithful and fearless servant of him? What might I be enduring at this present time that, if I will endure it with hope and perseverance, can help me become stronger and better on the other side of it?

References:
1. James 1:2–3.
2. Heb. 12:6.
3. John 16:33.
4. 2 Tim. 3:12.
5. Jer. 23:16.
6. 1 Pet. 3:17.
7. Rom. 8:28.
8. 1 Pet 5:10.
9. Jer. 3:27.
10. 1 Thess. 5:18.
11. Eph. 2:6–7.
12. Rom. 5:3–5.
13. 1 Pet. 5:8–9.
14. 2 Cor. 2:11.
15. Acts 17:27.
16. Ps. 34:18.
17. 2 Cor. 4:8–10.
18. Gen. 45:5, 8.
19. Phil. 2:13.

23

The World Was Not Worthy of Them

There have always been wonderful examples of faith. The scripture says,

> Therefore, since we are surrounded by such a great cloud of witnesses, let us throw off everything that hinders and the sin that so easily entangles. And let us run with perseverance the race marked out for us, fixing our eyes on Jesus, the pioneer and perfecter of faith.[1]

The world would have us believe that few live by faith and that, if we are living by faith, we are fairly alone. The world would have us believe that the intelligent modern generations live by knowledge and reason. But it simply is not so; everyone lives by faith. The reality is that most live life believing in a future that may not ever happen for them. In fact, it is arguable that all of what we believe to be truth is held only through faith or trust in information given to us by others—information believed to be truth but always with numerous facts left unchecked. We may believe it to be the truth; we don't ever, perhaps can't ever, know or prove it to be true, though. We ultimately can only *believe* it to be true. We receive it by faith.

Humanism is the religion that believes in and serves only humanity—the religion that would trust only in itself. It is the religion where humans live for and serve themselves. It manifests itself both in the religious and the nonreligious. It is nothing new. It started in the Garden at the fall of man into sin. In fact, it is merely the fruit of the wrong tree—the Tree of the Knowledge of Good and Evil. It seeks to eschew faith in the divine and trust only in human ingenuity. Much of religion, and even much of Christianity, are sometimes arguably quite humanistic.

Humanism—whether nonreligious or religious—holds that we are right (morally, religiously, sensibly) because we are right (correct, intelligent, informed). Atheistic humanism contends that humans can solve all our own problems, and that religion is but a crutch and to be considered generally destructive. In fact, the sixth assertion of Humanist Manifesto I states, "We are convinced that the time has passed for theism, deism, modernism, and the several varieties of 'new thought.'"[2] Humanism claims no faith but is, in fact, likely the most foolish faith of all—faith in humanity. The reality is that "it is better to take refuge in the Lord than to trust in humans,"[3] and, "Those who trust in themselves are fools, but those who walk in wisdom are kept safe."[4] Yes, religion—faith—has long been just one more thing corrupted by fallen humanity. The confusion of faith—from faith in God to faith in man—is the original sin that is at the root of all sin.

The Bible holds that we are right (declared righteous or right in God's sight) by a right faith—a complete trust in the right thing or person, that is, God. "For in the gospel the righteousness of God is revealed—a righteousness that is by faith from first to last, just as it is written: 'The righteous will live by faith.'"[5] We are made right by having faith—by believing in God's mercy and provision for us. And not by first believing what is right, but by believing (having faith in) *who* is right—God. We must believe it simply because it is the truth. It is reality. Theology should thus be about knowing God the most, not merely knowing the most about God.

Knowledge and reason alone can only produce a kind of intelligence. Such intelligence can, however, prove counterproductive to human well-being; in fact, it can be very destructive in certain instances. Calvin Coolidge, thirtieth president of the United States, 1923-1929, is credited by some as having said, "the world is full of educated derelicts." Human education often does not equate to increased wisdom; seemingly in some instances it actually squelches it. However, reasonable faith produces the ultimate intelligence—godly wisdom, and wisdom trumps mere human intelligence every time. "The fear of the Lord is the beginning of wisdom, and knowledge of the Holy One is understanding."[6] It is wisdom that allows knowledge to be useful and productive in the first place.

Unchecked religion is bad and can even be brutal; unchecked intelligence is just as bad and is generally futile. Unchecked religious humanism is even worse. In either case, humanity is god, for it is humanity that is worshiped and served. However, in effect, it's not all of humanity, because the poor and weaker peoples are mostly forgotten and left behind with the crumbs. It is the most powerful and wealthy classes of humanity that will ultimately be most served when God is not worshiped and humans are. On the other hand, reasonable faith—biblical faith—is wisdom and godliness personified in humanity. It is an instant check on religion and intelligence that would go askew and become self-serving. When the God of heaven is recognized as God, humanity aligns itself to worship him and to serve his purposes. Every human becomes valuable, and the weak and disadvantaged receive the greater attention.

But contrary to what the world wishes to be true and wishes us to believe, there are still plenty of faithful. There always have been. There are many examples of faithfulness; in fact, there is a "cloud of witnesses," as scripture says.

The specific "cloud of witnesses" referred to in Hebrews 12:1 are the ones spoken of in the chapter just before, Hebrews 11. Watching and envisioning believers like these, who boldly act with confidence in their faith, will inspire us to get rid of the things that hinder our own pursuits of Christ as well as the sins that entangle us and stymie our growth. We are wise to imitate others who also imitate Christ.[7] To do so, we must fix our own eyes on Jesus, so we will recognize in others the behaviors that look like him.

The faith of the faithful witnesses was and always will be expressed in the confidence of hope and assurance in the things of God we cannot see. Faith is thus described, "Now faith is confidence in what we hope for and assurance about what we do not see. This is what the ancients were commended for."[8] The faithful surely understood that "without faith, it is impossible to please God because anyone who comes to him must believe that he exists and that he rewards those who earnestly seek him."[9]

This listing of the faithful in Hebrews 11 begins with Abel, who was killed by his own brother because he had offered a sacrifice to God that God accepted, while his brother's was rejected.[10] Whether Abel's sacrifice was right in kind, manner, or motive is not directly described. But his brother's offering was rejected. Murder must have already been in Cain's heart, because Cain killed Abel, who is the first martyr recorded in scripture. Then there was Enoch, who walked so closely and faithfully with God that God simply took him, so he did not experience actual human death.[11] And it was Noah who built an ark, in preparation for an, at that time, unheard of rainstorm and subsequent flood that God warned him about.[12] It obviously took Noah and his family years of painstaking work and service to God while living in a world that had gone completely mad.[13] By their faith, they saved themselves, and they saved humanity.

But it was Abraham who is called the father of our faith. At God's command, he left his home and moved to a place far away that God led him to.[14] At an old age, he and his aged wife, Sarah, trusted God and gave birth, far past their childbearing years, to their son, Isaac, whom God had promised them. Through Isaac would descend a whole nation—the nation of Israel.[15] Abraham later prepared, per God's direct instructions, to offer this son God had given him upon an altar. However, mercifully and clearly by plan, God stopped him, but only after Abraham had fully demonstrated his complete faith in God by preparing for the commanded sacrifice.[16]

Isaac then faithfully blessed his own sons, Jacob and Esau, according to God's will for their futures.[17] Jacob, whose name was later changed to Israel, spawned the whole nation of God through his twelve sons, but blessed the two sons of Joseph, creating two tribes from him out of what would only have been one.[18] And Joseph believed that God would lead Israel out of Egypt and back to Canaan's Land, their Promised Land. Therefore, he gave instructions to his descendants that his bones were not to be left in Egypt, but that they should be taken to Canaan's Land when Israel departed Egypt.[19]

Moses's parents, at great risk to themselves, hid him for three months in order to save their son from the pharaoh's ordered infanticide because they knew God had chosen him as someone extraordinary. They risked their own lives by ignoring the order of the Egyptian pharaoh.[20] They also orchestrated for him to be adopted by the pharaoh's daughter in the king's palace. As he grew up, Moses then refused to identify with the pharaoh's house but rather saw himself as a leader of Israel. He chose to suffer with God's people, rather than to live in the lap of luxury as he could have. He fled the pharaoh, fearing his own execution for inadvertently killing an Egyptian while defending an Israelite. However, he returned to Egypt, at great risk, to face another equally powerful pharaoh in order to, at God's command, lead Israel out of Egypt.[21]

The whole nation of Israel dared to walk through the Red Sea via a canyon opened between two high water walls. How intimidating must that have been with the possibility of the water suddenly burying them? They, however, trusted God and walked on the dry seabed to freedom.[22] Over forty years later, they would conquer Jericho through another act of God—a highly unusual ritual of marching around the walled city for seven days and then finally shouting, as instructed, in order for the walls to simply fall outward.[23] A local prostitute was spared because she had blessed and protected the two scouts Joshua had sent to spy out Jericho.[24]

A number of others, along with their feats of faith, is mentioned. They had great successes in conquering kings, administering God's justice, and receiving his promises; they defied lions and fires and swords. God turned their weaknesses into strengths. Women saw their loved ones raised from the dead. They also suffered torture, were chained and imprisoned, and were jeered and flogged. Some were stoned, others were sawed in two, and still others were killed by the sword. They were ill clad, poor, persecuted, and mistreated. They wandered through all kinds of formidable terrain, living in caves and holes.[25] But still,

> All these people were still living by faith when they died. They did not receive the things promised; they only saw them and welcomed them from a distance, admitting that they were foreigners and strangers on earth. People who say such things show that they are looking for a country of their own. If they had been thinking of the country they had left, they would have had opportunity to return. Instead, they were longing for a better country—a heavenly one. Therefore, God is not ashamed to be called their God, for he has prepared a city for them.[26]

And because of their faith in God shown by their great and daring feats, as well as by their faithfulness even in suffering defeats and setbacks, the Bible says, "the world was not worthy of them."[27]

In every generation, there has always been a "cloud of witnesses," the multitudes of those who live by faith in the one God—Yahweh; a cloud of witnesses who confess and profess that his son, Jesus, is Lord.

The world, in its fallen state, is not worthy of them because, in its corrupted state, it is not worthy of Him.

Inspiration: Elijah, arguably the most powerful of the prophets, felt alone. And he felt like a failure. Plus, he was afraid and in hiding.[28] He had just carried out a great feat of faith for God in demonstrating Yahweh's power and showing Baal and Asherah as vain and useless idols. He and the Israelites executed the 850 false prophets that had amassed around these two idols, while serving Ahab and Jezebel, the corrupt king and queen.[29] Afterward, Elijah fled from Jezebel, who had pledged to kill him by the next day. Discouraged, he asked God to take his life, saying he was no better than his forefathers. He fell asleep only to be awakened and fed by an angel of the Lord. He got up, ate, and traveled to Horeb, the mountain of Yahweh. Then this happened:

> And the word of the Lord came to him: "What are you doing here, Elijah?" He replied, "I have been very zealous for the Lord God Almighty. The Israelites have rejected your covenant, torn down your altars, and put your prophets to death with the sword. I am the only one left, and now they are trying to kill me too."[30]

Most believers have at some point asked themselves, "What am I doing here?" Just as God had asked Elijah. Elijah reports to him the unfaithfulness of the Israelites and says he is the only one left. Many of us have also felt quite alone at times, especially those of us who are called to step out in faith to do tough things for God that few others will dare to do or are unable or not called to do. As he will with us, God let Elijah know that was not true. He tells Elijah to go back and anoint Hazael king over Aram, Jehu king over Israel, and Elisha as Elijah's prophet successor—that they will carry out his will.[31] Also, God says he has left seven thousand who have not bowed to and kissed Baal. God indeed had his "remnant" embedded in Israel.[32]

God seemingly always has had a remnant, albeit sometimes small, such as in the case of Noah and his family. God had, in the worst of times, reserved a remnant for himself in Israel. Similarly, God reserved a remnant in the church during its darkest centuries. And God surely still reserves a remnant even in weakening, unfaithful, or dying churches. Although they might be hard to see, they are there. And God will reveal them in his own time: "For there must also be factions among you, that those who are approved may be recognized among you."[33] The remnant of those approved by God will ultimately be recognized though. When we are living by faith in God, we can be assured that we are not alone. No matter how it seems, we never are. There is always a cloud of witnesses that have gone before us and live in the world with us. There will surely be many more to follow until Christ returns. These are those of whom the world is not worthy and that the world groans awaiting their revelation.[34] Constant awareness of the cloud of faithful witnesses will spur us as well to live lives that are worthy of the gospel of Christ.[35]

Prayer: Father, help me to live a life worthy of the gospel, a life which the world is not worthy of but that we are all still offered, because of your great love and mercy for us all. May I grow in a faith like all those who have called on your name, lived worthy of the gospel, and brought honor and glory to you, the one and only King.

Reflection: If my faith were to be written about by a prophet of God, what would be said of it? What would I want them to be able to write? What strengthens my faith most? What weakens my faith the most? What steps do I want to take moving forward? Who can I get to help me?

References:
1. Heb. 12:1.
2. *Humanist Manifesto I*, "The New Humanist," United States: American Humanist Association, 1933.
3. Ps. 118:8.
4. Prov. 28:26.
5. Rom. 1:17.
6. Prov. 9:10.
7. 1 Cor. 11:1.
8. Heb. 11:1–2.
9. Heb. 11:6.
10. Heb. 11:4.
11. Heb. 11:5-6.
12. Heb. 11:7.
13. Gen. 6:5.
14. Heb. 11:8-10.
15. Heb. 11:11-12.
16. Heb. 11:17-19.
17. Heb. 11:20.

18. Heb. 11:21.
19. Heb. 11:22.
20. Heb. 11:23.
21. Heb. 11:24-28.
22. Heb. 11:29.
23. Heb. 11:30.
24. Heb. 11:31.
25. Heb. 11:32-38.
26. Heb. 11:13-16.
27. Heb. 11:38.
28. 1 Kings 19.
29. 1 Kings 18.
30. 1 Kings 19:9–10.
31. 1 Kings 19:15–17.
32. 1 Kings 19:18.
33. 1 Cor. 11:19.
34. Rom. 8:19.
35. Phil. 1:27.

24

Satan's Great Deception: That Faith Can Exist Without Obedience

Jesus asked a question to those who claimed to follow him but were not obeying him: "But why do you call Me 'Lord, Lord,' and not do the things which I say?"[1] It is a question all disciples need to ask themselves occasionally. To call Jesus "Lord" and yet not obey him is contradictory and duplicitous. But humans have always found ways to justify their duplicity to themselves: "How long will you falter between two opinions?"[2]

Humans can be notoriously ambivalent. And that ambivalence can certainly often be seen in our faith in various ways. Why is it we would claim to believe a thing and then behave as though we do not? Why is it that we claim one thing and then do another? Who are we trying to fool? Who do we think we are fooling? Who ends up being the real fool?

Jesus spoke of those among us as "believers" whom, on the last day, he will reject. However, he says these people will still claim, in their incredulity and defiance, to have performed great deeds for Christ—"prophesied, driven out demons, performed miracles." But Jesus sees these he is speaking of very differently. In his final analysis and judgment, he says that his response to them will be, "I never knew you. Away from me, you evildoers!"[3] These are chilling words that should get the attention of all Christians.

There have always been those who would tell us that we can have faith in God and not necessarily seek to align ourselves with his will. It is a shallow and useless faith that acts as though grace itself is cheap. It claims to believe God, but it is not made evident in the necessary corresponding behavior. Satan is behind it every time, reinforcing it with his original lie: "You will not surely die."[4] James, the brother of Jesus, scoffed at the notion that there could be duplicity in genuine faith, saying, "But be doers of the word, and not hearers only, deceiving yourselves."[5] Hearing the faithful words of the Lord telling us to do certain things and behave in certain ways should prompt an immediate response on our part to give our best effort to obey him. However, if our faith does not prompt such an honest effort in responding, we are deceiving ourselves indeed!

James further sought to correct a view among early Christians. He was likely addressing Jewish Christians who might have seen Christianity, with its message of grace, as an excuse for disobedience and a release from guilt.[6] "What good is it, my brothers and sisters, if someone claims to have faith but has no deeds? Can such faith save them?"[7] Faith without the corresponding action is contradictory. "In the same way, faith by itself, if it is not accompanied by action, is dead."[8] A disobedient faith, be it disobedience by action or by inaction, has no life in it.

However, we might claim to believe anyway. But James would counter, "You believe that there is one God. Good! Even the demons believe that—and shudder."[9] In the final analysis, James summarizes, saying, "As the body without the spirit is dead, so faith without deeds is dead."[10]

Yes, it may be said that we are saved through our faith in Jesus alone, but only if faith is properly defined as scripture defines it.[11] Yet that final word, "alone," is added to the expression to better stress that we are in no way saved by any deserving act of our own. "Alone," however, is not in any scripture. If not very, very careful, some might echo some not-so-honest words, "You will not surely die," so as to suggest that it matters not how disobedient you may be, and that your faith *alone* saves you, generally meaning some "faith moment." And still, the reality is that faith itself does not save us; God saves us. We have faith that he saves us. Justification is his justifying our sins through his goodness and grace, not our justifying our disobedience through logic or with our hearts, our words, or what we believe to be true.

"What shall we say, then? Shall we go on sinning so that grace may increase? By no means! We are those who have died to sin; how can we live in it any longer?"[12] How ridiculous the faith that believes grace is somehow a justification for disobedience, be it in things we are expected not to do but continue to do or in things we are supposed to do but we don't. Nor is grace an excuse for complacency, apathy, or any other presumption on God's grace.

The apostle John, the great apostle of love and life, says, "Now by this we know that we know Him if we keep His commandments. He who says, 'I know Him,' and does not keep His commandments is a liar, and the truth is not in him."[13] John does not mince words in addressing those futile thinkers who might scoff at any connection between faith and obedience. In trying to defend against Christian doctrines that suggest or infer that we somehow earn God's grace by our works and behavior, these can overcorrect and lead others to believe that obedience does not factor in at all. He calls those who claim to know God but who are disobedient "liars"! Our faith is, in fact, shown and defined by our obedience to God's guidance. Faith is best seen in action consistent with what our faith implies, and it is the only true testimony to the genuineness of our faith other than God's own testimony.

Further, John writes, "But if anyone obeys his word, love for God is truly made complete in them. This is how we know we are in him: Whoever claims to live in him must live as Jesus did."[14] An authentic faith in Jesus will clearly be manifested in the lifestyle of the true disciple. Anything else is simply a contradiction. There is no inconsistency in the faith that is evident by action. There is, however, a gross inconsistency in the faith that is claimed but not demonstrated by action.

The Bible knows nothing of a faith that is separate from obe-dience. Legalism and its works are about faith in oneself, the fruit of the tree that brings only death. It is of self-reliance, not reliance on God at all. It is the faith and religion of humanism in its many forms—theistic and atheistic.

Faith is much more than mental ascent, however. The scrip-tures would have nothing to do with such, because Jesus will have nothing to do with such: "Why do you call me 'Lord, Lord,' and not do the things which I say?" Obedience is not about show. Obedience is not about performance. Obedience is not about earning anything. Obedience is not about perfection. Rather, obedience is about direction. The servant will easily be seen to be following the direction of his master. The disciple will clearly be seen going in the same direction as her teacher. Indeed, the reality is that much of the task commanded to us is to show God's perfection through our own imperfections, to show his power through our weakness, and to show his goodness through our lack of goodness. Paul writes,

> But God, who is rich in mercy, because of His great love with which He loved us, even when we were dead in tres-passes, made us alive together with Christ (by grace you have been saved) and raised us up together and made us sit together in the heavenly places in Christ Jesus, that in the ages to come, He might show the exceeding riches of His grace in His kindness toward us in Christ Jesus.[15]

It is a stated purpose of ours that in Christ Jesus, we allow God's incomparable grace to be on display in our lives as it is expressed to us in the kindness he shows us. We are not here, saved in Christ, because we are somehow good; we are here because he is good: "For we are His workmanship, created in Christ Jesus for good works, which God prepared beforehand that we should walk in them."[16] "Let your light so shine before men, that they may see your good works and glorify your Father in heaven."[17]

Of course, we are saved because of our faith in his grace and goodness and not faith in our own.[18] There can be no valid biblical argument to the contrary. It is utterly ridiculous to believe we could be saved any other way, as history has well recorded the depths of human depravity and our utter inability to alleviate the painful lesions humanity received from the Fall.

Yet there can neither be any valid argument to the contrary concerning the utter inconsistency of a faith that would be claimed but not manifested in the zealous attempt to serve and obey the Lord we claim.[19] Again, "Why do you call me Lord and not do as I ask?"

Saving faith will always be manifested. It can't not be. A changed belief (from belief in self or others to a belief in God) will lead to a changed mind (repentance). A changed mind will inevitably lead to changed behaviors.

A faith that does not manifest fervent attempts at obedience can in no way be a saving faith, period. That's why we need to regularly check ourselves and ask how we can call Jesus Lord and not give our best effort at obeying him, as any good servant naturally will.

Inspiration: Jesus told a story to demonstrate the contradiction of a claimed faith that is not evident through obedience:

What do you think? There was a man who had two sons. He went to the first and said, "Son, go and work today in the vineyard." "I will not," he answered, but later he changed his mind and went. Then, the father went to the other son and said the same thing. He answered, "I will, sir," but he did not go. Which of the two did what his father wanted? "The first," they answered. Jesus said to them, "Truly I tell you, the tax collectors and the prostitutes are entering the kingdom of God ahead of you. For John came to you to show you the way of righteousness, and you did not believe him, but the tax collectors and the prostitutes did. And even after you saw this, you did not repent and believe him."[20]

One of the sons said he would obey but did not (duplicity at least, hypocrisy at worst). The other said he would not obey but then changed his mind (repented) and did. The moral of Jesus's story might be summarized as, "talk is cheap, and actions speak louder than words." Jesus's call to grace through faith does not merely free us from the guilt of our sin; it frees us from our sin itself. We no longer have to live in it. We are called to faithful obedience because what we are asked to do is what we were originally designed to do. The apostle Paul wrote, "For the grace of God has appeared that offers salvation to all people. It teaches us to say no to ungodliness and worldly passions, and to live self-controlled, upright, and godly lives in this present age"[21] The grace of God not only extends forgiveness to us; it teaches us how to live faithfully. Genuine faith will always drive one toward obedience.

Prayer: Lord, lead me in the faith that is not merely spoken but in the faith that is fully expressed and professed in a life worthy of the gospel. May I never be the shallow and vain soul that presumes some entitlement to your precious grace and mercy, but rather may I be the humble servant who lives out an expressed debt of gratitude for the matchless grace you have poured out on us in Christ Jesus.

Reflection: Is my faith clearly expressed in a life lived in imitation of Jesus? How so? Where does the foundation of my faith need shored up? Where might duplicity be sneaking into my expression of faith?

References:
1. Luke 6:46.
2. 1 Kings 18:21.
3. Matt. 7:21–23.
4. Gen. 3:4.
5. James 1:22.
6. Rom. 6:1–2.
7. James 2:14.
8. James 2:17.

9. James 2:19.
10. James 2:26.
11. Rom. 5:1–11.
12. Rom. 6:1–2.
13. 1 John 2:3–4.
14. 1 John 2:5–6.
15. Eph. 2:4–7.
16. Eph. 2:10.
17. Matt. 5:16.
18. Eph. 2:8–9.
19. Rom. 12:11.
20. Matt. 21:28–32.
21. Titus 2:11–12.

25

God Acts When We Act

"Then he [Jesus] said to her, 'Daughter, your faith has healed you. Go in peace.'"[1] Also, "Then he [Jesus] said to him, 'Rise and go; your faith has made you well.'"[2] Your faith has healed you; your faith has made you well. "Your faith"? It has made you well? Really? Is it not God who did it? Yes? No? Maybe? Might faith itself, working within each of us, have its own inherent power because of who we are and how we are made?

Jesus's work within humanity was, and seemingly still is, apparently limited in some way to the extent that we have faith in him. Matthew tells us, "And he did not do many miracles there because of their lack of faith."[3] Perhaps it was because he was unwilling to work in those with little faith in him. Perhaps our lack of faith disables what he can do for us because of how he designed us in the first place. Either way, our faith is most assuredly essential in accessing many of God's blessings.

Suffice it to say, our faith in him is a big deal to God, not only as a deciding factor of our very salvation, but also regarding if and how much he can work in us. Salvation is by faith from beginning to end, not just in the beginning and not just in the end.

There is tremendous power for us in *what* we believe in and, as well, how strongly and genuinely we believe in it. We act most confidently in the things we are convinced are true and right. Jesus said, "Everything is possible for one who believes."[4]

"Everything" includes a lot of things. "Possible" means nothing is impossible. The ending phrase, "For the one who believes," tells us where the power is and, thus, in whom we should believe.

Powerful possibilities open up to us by our believing—believing in and doing good or believing in and even doing evil; believing in God or in ourselves. We simply find a power within ourselves when we strongly believe something to be true. We find the power for what we think we should do in what we believe to be true.

But how much faith is that? What metrics are to be used to measure or describe faith? The degree of our certainty? Confidence in our ability? Confidence in God's ability? Assurance of God's willingness to empower us? Or what, exactly? Further, what measures, if there be any, might be used to quantify any of these?

Truth or fact is simply what we say that we know but what in reality we only think and feel with the greatest conviction. And it is the things we claim to know that we act most confidently on. What, however, is the distinction between knowing and believing? Humans have long speculated and philosophized about it all. Seemingly the answer for many ends up falling into an abyss of subjectivism (i.e., what I think or feel). Out of exasperation at merely trying to think about it, many simply avoid or give up on the discussion. But, there is grave danger in subjectivism because of the deceptiveness of the human heart when it depends only on itself.[5] Equally dangerous is settling for avoidance and ignorance of key life topics. The former is to fly without map or compass; the latter is to fly blindly. At best, a wrong destination will be arrived at. At worst, a deadly crash is in the offing.

For the Bible, knowledge begins and ends with God. Jesus Christ is the Alpha and the Omega, the beginning and the end.[6] He *is* the "I AM." "'Very truly I tell you,' Jesus answered, 'before Abraham was born, I am!'"[7] He is the original and eternal existence that brings all other things that exist.[8] All that exists begins and ends with him; thus, all knowledge begins and ends with him. He is truth—pure truth, period.

However, humanism, the ultimate fruit of the Tree of the Knowledge of Good and Evil, suggests another formula: that humanity did not come from God at all, but that "God" came from humanity; that is, we made the divine up. And further, since we made up our "god" to serve our own purposes, we can also ignore such an idol god in order to serve these same personally derived desires. But the real subversive point of this deceptive fruit is the assertion that we don't need God; and thus, we need to *be* God: "You will be like God," Satan lied.[9] And humanity keeps believing the lie over and over and over, to the demise of most of humanity.

To have any sensible construct about knowledge, we must determine where the knowledge is originally derived. Is there knowledge that is objective and independent of us, or is knowledge subjective and dependent on us?

The Bible is clear on the matter. Truth—the ultimate knowledge—is derived from God. Jesus, as he emanates from God, calls himself "the truth."[10] Thus, in the biblical story, faith is believing with certainty what we deem to be *the* truth, who for Christians is Yahweh and his earthly emanation—his son, Jesus Christ, Emmanuel, meaning "God with us."

And God has somehow made his actions on and in us contingent upon our beliefs and actions toward him and through him. This is about our faith in him, not our faith in ourselves or others. Jesus said, "Truly I tell you, if you have faith as small as a mustard seed, you can say to this mountain, 'Move from here to there,' and it will move."[11] Hence, it can be suggested that having faith in God is contingent not on possessing *great* faith, but on possessing a *little* faith in a great God!

Yes, faith in ourselves or in others can potentially unleash tremendous here-and-now human power. However, that kind of faith in what is *human* must be big and powerful to have much effect. In contrast, only a very small amount of faith in God—in fact, the size of a tiny mustard seed—can unleash limitless power. In a discussion about how anyone could possibly even be saved, given its seeming difficulty, Jesus told the first disciples, "With man, this is impossible, but with God, all things are possible."[12] Women and men might presently have the human potential to do amazing things without God's intervention (and that potential is from God as well, as that is how he created us), but without God, it is still quite limited. Some things are just impossible for us. However, God's potential is unlimited.

God chose through Christ to make a great mystery known to all who would believe, which is, "Christ in you [us], the hope of glory."[13] We can, on our own, do a little; God can, though us, do a lot though. In fact, Paul says, God "is able to do immeasurably more than all we ask or imagine, according to his power that is at work within us."[14] God can do immeasurably more through us than we could even dream of doing on our own, and it is according to the power of his Spirit that he has put in us as believers. The gospel message itself is more than we can ask or imagine. Who could honestly ask another to die in his or her place for a crime the other did not commit? Who could then ask that same person to forgive them for the repetitive and innumerable sins and neglect that have been continually committed against such a sacrificial soul over one's lifetime? Yet, that is what the gospel tells us God will do for us if we will live by faith in him—he will forgive us over and over if we will but put our faith in him.

Yes, all that is to be accomplished is to ultimately be accomplished through faith—in ourselves or in God. God has designed it that way. With a lot of faith in ourselves, we can do some pretty amazing things. However, with just a little faith in God, we can do a whole, whole lot more!

Inspiration: She is known as the "bleeding woman" or, from an older Bible translation, the "woman with the issue of blood." Matthew, Mark, and Luke all tell of her.[15] She is the individual who was not healed by a touch from Jesus; rather, she was the one who had reached out in the crowd to touch him; at least, she touched his garment. It is assumed she was bleeding vaginally, but unlike regular menstruation, her bleeding was constant, and it had been going on for twelve years! She was surely anemic and emaciated. She was obviously desperate. Who wouldn't be?

Mark bluntly writes that "she had suffered a great deal under the care of many doctors and had spent all she had; yet instead of getting better, she had gotten worse."[16] By Jewish ritual law, she was unclean and could not touch another. She was in violation of their law simply by mingling in the crowd.

The Jews, clearly believed that all healing was from God.[17] One Jewish writing stated: "It was neither herb nor mollifying plaister [sic] that cured them, but thy word, O Lord, which healeth all things."[18] Those from the ancient East had other views, however, as demonstrated by one of their proverbs: "Have faith, though it be only in a stone, and you will recover."[19] The earliest physicians mentioned in the Bible are those in Egypt, and they were of a priestly class of physicians who are mentioned in the story of Joseph.[20] As well, there were physicians who practiced medicine in the Greek world, with Hippocrates being the most famous. And there were also those who were practicing forms of medicine in Israel. However, with their crude, uninformed, undeveloped, and often even superstitious practices, those who suffered chronic diseases and had the means to do so often called on one physician after another looking for a cure, and they potentially suffered as much from their treatments as from the diseases themselves.

The woman of Jesus's story was one such person. She had surely heard of Jesus and determined that if perhaps she could only surreptitiously touch his garment, she could be healed. And she was right! She was healed immediately as soon as she touched only his garment. And, likely to her chagrin and embarrassment, Jesus also knew it. He knew something had happened: "Jesus realized that power had gone out from him."[21] He turned and called her out on it. After she identified herself, Jesus told her, "Daughter, your faith has healed you. Go in peace and be freed from your suffering." Somehow her faith had activated something in the power of God, as found in Christ, which flowed into her and made her right again. It is God who makes us right in the first place, and he can make us right again and again after this world has messed us up. Her faith in God somehow engaged

God, and she was made well. And for this one person amid all the others mentioned, she was healed—not on a day when Jesus Christ touched her, but on the day she touched him, as described in the concluding two verses of a poem, "Touching God," written by this author a few years back about the bleeding woman.

> I lived out my life; got my family back,
> The day I risked all to touch the Messiah,
> Such a simple touch, in desperation for sure,
> Ended my life as a broken, rejected pariah!
>
> So the day I was healed, I remember so well,
> I was desperate, not proper and prim,
> But it was not the day that God touched me,
> It was the day I reached out and touched him!

Prayer: Father, I reach out now not in secretiveness or fear, as the bleeding woman, but I reach out to touch you in faith. I want to find you, to know you, and to be in constant contact with you. Heal me inside and out with your divine power, and make me a healing balm of yours for others who, through me, would also reach out to touch you.

Reflection: Do I believe that there is a certain power, separate and apart from any direct act of God, to be found in simply believing in something (a certain amount of power in faith itself)? Why or why not? Do I believe that my faith in God will serve as a prompt of sorts that can in some way activate his power to work in me and those I love? Do I trust God to do things that I alone do not have the capacity to bring about? How might I "touch" God in such a way? Do I trust that God's purpose will prevail in my life and in the world he created?

References:
1. Luke 8:48.
2. Luke 17:19.
3. Matt. 13:58.

4. Mark 9:23.

5. Jer. 17:9.

6. Rev. 22:13.

7. John 8:58.

8. John 1:1–4; Col. 1:16.

9. Gen. 3:4.

10. John 14:6.

11. Matt. 17:20.

12. Matt. 19:26.

13. Col. 1:27.

14. Eph. 3:20.

15. Matt. 9:20–22; Mark 5:25–34; Luke 8:43–48.

16. Mark 5:26.

17. Deut. 32:39.

18. Wisd. of Sol. 16:12.

19. Wight, Fred. *Manners and Customs of Biblical Lands.* Chicago: Moody Bible Institute, 1953. http://www.baptistbiblebelievers.com/OTStudies/MannersandCustomsInBibleLands1953.aspx, p. 97.

20. Gen. 50:2, 26.

21. Mark 5:30.

Conclusion:

Unbelief Is of the Heart

Arguably, unbelief is not so much from the mind, although it will end up there and be justified by any number of arguments, but unbelief originates in a deceived and deceptive heart. To whatever degree unbelief may be of the mind, ultimately, it sets itself up and festers deeply within our hearts. It becomes a stronghold there. It can incapacitate the mind's objectivity and convince us that, in our unbelief, we are thinking and feeling reasonably and logically. It can make us feel that we have no agenda other than reason and truth. But in reality, reason and truth have lost their grips within us.

So, as the Holy Spirit says: "Today, if you hear his voice, do not harden your hearts as you did in the rebellion, during the time of testing in the wilderness, where your ancestors tested and tried me, though for forty years they saw what I did. That is why I was angry with that generation; I said, 'Their hearts are always going astray, and they have not known my ways.' So I declared on oath in my anger, 'They shall never enter my rest.'"[1]

Their hearts went astray, thus they could not know God's way—the truth. Unbelief of this kind is not some fatal emotional thought that we are powerless to dispel though. It is, in fact, something we can and must do something about if we are to objectively pursue truth.

See to it, brothers and sisters, that none of you has a sinful, unbelieving heart that turns away from the living God. But encourage one another daily, as long as it is called "today," so that none of you may be hardened by sin's deceitfulness. We have come to share in Christ, if indeed we hold our original conviction firmly to the very end.[2]

An unbelieving heart becomes a sinful heart. An unbelieving heart ultimately sets adrift one's life into a sea of purposelessness and selfishness. Unbelief is based on the assumption from the deceptive fruit of the Tree of the Knowledge of Good and Evil. Unbelievers must go it alone without God, believing that they can, as the serpent told Eve, be like God themselves, knowing what good and evil is. Such unbelief is, at its core, a choice, albeit often a fairly unconscious one. We feel the life God breathed into us—the inner spirit—battling against our flesh and fleshly natures that would live by instinct and the simple desires and wants—often brute instincts. Yet within us, "The Spirit himself testifies with our spirit that we are God's children."[3] But still, in fear and doubt, we give way to a sinful, unbelieving heart. We trust only in ourselves and in those of a similar ilk. Ultimately, however, we trust in no one and nothing to any significant degree.

Thus, it is most important that we address faith early and often in our lives and in the lives of our children and others we influence. We must be encouraged, and we must, on a daily basis, encourage others toward spiritual, mental, and emotional sanity. We must not allow a hardened heart—the gangrene of the soul—to set up within us, destroying the very fiber of our living being.

"Today, if you hear his voice, do not harden your hearts as you did in the rebellion." Who were they who heard and rebelled? Were they not all those Moses led out of Egypt? And with whom was he angry for forty years? Was it not with those who sinned, whose bodies perished in the wilderness? And to whom did God swear that they would never enter his rest if not to those who disobeyed? So we see that they were not able to enter, because of their unbelief.[4]

Israel hardened her heart against God, and rather than find the truth of God, the people of Israel discovered only the truth of their sinful natures and, thus, did as their evil desires demanded. They made their nation and themselves into their gods. Their expectation of the Messiah thus became self-serving. They rebelled, and God allowed the inner infection of their unbelief to spread to the whole nation, and a whole generation died, lost and wandering in a barren wilderness. Their unbelief inevitably caused their disobedience. Their disobedience kept them from entering the Promised Land for forty years. It was the same unbelief that caused them to reject the Messiah when he came. Emmanuel (God with us) was among them, yet as a nation, they completely rejected him. For us, unbelief keeps us from finding and experiencing the glorious truth of God in Christ Jesus and, thus, from inclusion in the Kingdom of God.

Theirs is a biblical story of tragedy. We must learn from them, or we will follow them down the same tragic path of unbelief of the heart. Jesus said many, even among active Christians, would.

Some unbelief is due to negative emotions. For example, we may find the whole idea of believing in the unseen as too frustrating and difficult. Or we may be turned off by how we perceive religion, justifiably or unjustifiably. Our negative response may be against, as we view it, the shallowness, the dishonesty, or the pretentiousness of religion in general. Or it may be a reaction to others we know who believe in God and disappoint or disillusion us. Perhaps a bad experience or two has turned us off or made us angry. Maybe we grew up going to church, and we perceive our experiences as less than desirable or downright bad. Unfortunately, many tend to generalize to God and to all Christians what may be a justifiable distaste to some individual or because of some unpleasant experience(s) or incident(s).

We also might simply find ourselves angry with God when he does not give us the answers we desire and that we feel we should have; or because the world's design is not as we would have it; or because God is not who we think he should be or does not act the way we think is right. We could be angry with God because of disappointments such as the deaths of loved ones or the loss of our own health. We might become bitter because God did not give us the thing(s) we desired and fervently asked him for. The emotions will vary, but if we do not take great care, the results will be the same—the unbelief of a hardened heart. Anger is certainly a common cause of it, but other emotions can be just as precipitous to our unbelief—being hurt, feeling betrayed, feeling ignored, getting disappointed, and becoming frustrated because of unmet expectations are just a few.

Some unbelief sets up in us because we cannot believe for some seemingly overpowering reason, be it emotional or intellectual. Or it might happen because we may not want to accept a certain belief because of its potential cost to us or others. It may begin with a seed of reason—in the mind—but ultimately, unbelief always establishes itself in the heart at the deepest levels. Thus, we will have negative emotions about the very idea of belief in the divine.

And at some points in all our lives and in various ways, unbelief will become an inner malady we must face. Sixteenth-century French theologian and Protestant reformer John Calvin said, "A perfect faith is nowhere to be found, so it follows that all of us are partly unbelievers." The reality is that there is the potential for unbelief to take root in any of our hearts. It is an inner force just waiting for its button to be pressed; it is the door beckoning us to a bad place, and it is just waiting to be opened.

As has already been considered earlier, the apostle Paul stated clearly the most basic biblical premise for belief in God, writing, "For since the creation of the world, God's invisible qualities—his eternal power and divine nature—have been clearly seen, being understood from what has been made, so that people are without excuse."[5] Thus, based on this premise, his conclusion about unbelievers was,

For although they knew God, they neither glorified him as God nor gave thanks to him, but their thinking became futile and their foolish hearts were darkened. Although they claimed to be wise, they became fools and exchanged the glory of the immortal God for images made to look like a mortal human being and birds and animals and reptiles.[6]

Their thinking became futile, and their hearts were darkened—that is, the inner light went off. Futile thinking causes heart problems—inner darkness, hardness, anger, anxiety, and so on. Thus, in claiming to be wise, we can become the biggest fools of all.

For the message of the cross is foolishness to those who are perishing, but to us who are being saved, it is the power of God. For it is written: "I will destroy the wisdom of the wise; the intelligence of the intelligent I will frustrate." Where is the wise person? Where is the teacher of the law? Where is the philosopher of this age? Has not God made foolish the wisdom of the world? For since, in the wisdom of God the world through its wisdom did not know him, God was pleased through the foolishness of what was preached to save those who believe…For the foolishness of God is wiser than human wisdom, and the weakness of God is stronger than human strength.[7]

The history of humankind is wrought with tragic beliefs, choices, decisions, and actions; much of it is caused by our inner beliefs and unbelief. Religion, of course, will have been discovered to be a root cause of many things, both good and bad. Of course, faith issues will play a role in most human problems. The first murder—Cain killing his brother Abel—was over religion. What else could and would kindle such passion? Thus, when faith becomes misguided, trouble or even tragedy is inevitable. But to deny God because of misguided souls or societies is subjectivity and illogic at their worst.

The home is said to be the most violent place on earth. Of course, it is where much violence occurs because that is where people spend much of their time. And the home is where people have the most access to each other. Within the family is where we are principally shaped and where certain behaviors are encouraged or discouraged. Emotions are powerful within family units. The love within a family, even the more instinctive "family love" (*storge* in Greek), can ignite fiery passions in the misguided or unstable. However, although we may, at times, desire to, we do not—simply cannot—stop believing in, deny the existence of, or abandon altogether marriage and family. But in spite of all the problems associated with marriage and family, we generally recognize the family unit as the foundation of civilization and seek to better it rather than destroy it. Efforts to get rid of family units as we know them will always end badly.

In another text concerning the mind-heart connection, Paul addresses this thought process of unbelief that leads to heart problems,

> So I tell you this, and insist on it in the Lord, that you must no longer live as the Gentiles do, in the futility of their thinking. They are darkened in their understanding and separated from the life of God because of the ignorance that is in them due to the hardening of their hearts. Having lost all sensitivity, they have given themselves over to sensuality, so as to indulge in every kind of impurity, and they are full of greed.[8]

Paul's reasoning is this: futile (ineffective) living comes from futile thinking; futile thinking—separation from the life of God because of ignorance of the divine—comes from a hardening of the heart. Although it may be reasoned by the mind, unbelief always resides in the heart, darkening and then hardening it. It never stops; it always continues to spiral out of control. To make matters worse, the heart is what controls our behavior: "Above all else, guard your heart, for everything you do flows from it."[9]

Behavior then just gets worse and worse; evil becomes the rule rather than the exception. Corruption finally destroys whatever it is allowed to feed on. A soul, as well as a whole society, can reach the point of no return in its slavery to sin and evil. And as the aforementioned Edmund Burke once observed, "Liberty does not exist in the absence of morality." Or as the apostle Paul asks rhetorically, "Don't you know that when you offer yourselves to someone as obedient slaves, you are slaves of the one you obey—whether you are slaves to sin, which leads to death, or to obedience, which leads to righteousness?"[10]

The reality is that Satan blinds the minds of unbelievers and they cannot understand the principle Paul was discussing. When we are unbelievers, we have always been blind. All we have ever known as inner "vision" is the sad groping and feeling of a darkened heart and the misleading illogic of a deceived mind. "Follow your heart" is the dark world's mantra. Because when unbelievers follow their hearts, Satan can lead them to destruction. Sadly, the heart, without the light of the Holy Spirit, is dark and blind. Therefore, it is helpless against the spiritual forces of evil. We can never really see until we allow faith and the light of the Holy Spirit to light the darkness and enable our eyes to finally be opened!

Our narrow minded, simplistic, and likely self-centered views of God are generally what set us up for unbelief. Unbelief is the inner, heart-level decision to deny, ignore, or otherwise disregard God. In the end, unbelief is not caused primarily by a logical, reasonable, objective decision against God's existence. These may be used to justify unbelief, but it is not the cause; the cause is an unconscious a priori decision made to simply disregard God because of our feelings about him or perhaps because of belief's implications to us. We can deny these inner motives, but simply denying them does not make them less real or make them disappear. We can justify these inner motives, but the truth is the truth, no matter what my motives are, no matter what I want to believe, the way I feel things should be, or what I finally insist the truth is. The objective truth and reality of the universe exists completely independent of any one of us. We can only discover it; we cannot mold it to our own liking.

To break things down a bit more, there is what might be thought of as *disbelief,* or doubt. And then there is *unbelief.* Unbelief may exist simply because the truth has never been heard or thought about. It is not necessarily a determined rejection of faith, but it is merely an absence of it. No decision has been made to the contrary of faith. Disbelief however is a decision against faith. It may or may not be short-term because of various intellectual issues, or it may precipitate from more experiential reasons. Disbelief is about something we simply cannot believe for whatever reasons. For the honest person, we simply do not believe. The apostle Thomas is an example of understandable disbelief. After the other apostles reported to him that the resurrected Christ had appeared, John reported Jesus appeared again with Thomas present:

> A week later, his disciples were in the house again, and Thomas was with them. Though the doors were locked, Jesus came and stood among them and said, "Peace be with you!" Then he said to Thomas, "Put your finger here; see my hands. Reach out your hand and put it into my side. Stop doubting and believe." Thomas said to him, "My Lord and my God!"[11]

Thomas went from disbelief to belief because he saw and touched the resurrected Christ, something that was seemingly unbelievable to him prior to the experience. His belief in Christ as Lord and Savior came about because of his changed mind, but his confession clearly erupted from a heart given over fully to belief. John continues, "Then Jesus told him, 'Because you have seen me, you have believed; blessed are those who have not seen and yet have believed.'"[12] Unbelief is also to remedied when one comes to hear the compelling reasons to believe in Jesus Christ as Lord and Savior

It never ceases to amaze the extreme efforts humanity will go to in order to disbelieve the existence of God and the minimal effort given to objectively exploring the reasons to believe. However beliefs that are based on merely what we *want* to believe, be it either believing or not believing in God, are propped up by emotion and therefore any discussion of faith will elicit more emotion than rationale. Belief often requires us to believe what we cannot understand. It often requires us to admit things that will make us, as believers, stand out as different. It can lead to social or intellectual disparagement. Whatever we believe, if it is at all important, will have a cost attached to it. But the truth is the truth, whether we believe it or not.

Disbelief can quickly mutate from honest nonacceptance to dishonest nonacceptance; from pure motives to impure motives; from objectivity to subjectivity; from reasonable and intellectual disbelief to unreasonable, less-than-truly-intellectual disbelief.

The Bible simply begins with God: "In the beginning, God created the heavens and the earth."[13] And it ends with God: "I am the Alpha and the Omega, the first and the last, the beginning and the end."[14] Scripture assumes God without attempting to prove his existence, likely because it assumes that the existence of a creation as marvelously made as ours necessitates the belief in a creator God. Anything less is, in the Bible's logic, morally and intellectually inexcusable: "For since the creation of the world, God's invisible qualities—his eternal power and divine nature—have been clearly seen, being understood from what has been made, so that people are without excuse."[15] Unbelief is without excuse.

It is stated bluntly by the psalmist, "The fool says in his heart, 'There is no God.'"[16] The Bible makes it clear that the creation is for and about its creator: "For in him all things were created: things in heaven and on earth, visible and invisible, whether thrones or powers or rulers or authorities; all things have been created through him and for him."[17] He made it all, and he rules it all. And it will all end up the way he plans. Christ created the world, and he sustains it: "The Son is the radiance of God's glory and the exact representation of his being, sustaining all things by his powerful word."[18] And yet science still wonders how the universe holds together.

Disbelief might suggest that the world has always existed, even though the best science available says it all started when pure energy became matter—that it had a beginning. Disbelief might suggest a self-generated world, even though science's own laws of cause and effect and thermodynamics would indicate it is impossible. Some in science might suggest that much about the universe will never be understood, even though the Bible has long given an explanation of where it all started and who it is that does, indeed, understand it all from beginning to end. Noted scientist, writer, and thinker Robert Jastrow summed it up this way in a 1982 interview with *Christianity Today*:

> Astronomers now find they have painted themselves into a corner because they have proven, by their own methods, that the world began abruptly in an act of creation to which you can trace the seeds of every star, every planet, every living thing in this cosmos and on the earth. And they have found that all this happened as a product of forces they cannot hope to discover. That there are what I or anyone would call supernatural forces at work is now, I think, a scientifically proven fact.[19]

That the universe is created by supernatural forces, i.e. God, is "a scientifically proven fact." Hmm.

Science seems to often suggest, wittingly or unwittingly, that it, and perhaps even it alone, will finally find all the answers we need. It might suggest that it alone is reasonable and that only it can be trusted. However, by its own admission, it cannot figure out where or what 95 percent of the matter and energy in the universe even is. Science would suggest humanity came into existence through billions of years of inorganic then organic causes and effects, mutations, and adaptations. And all of these obviously occur in certain ways and to various degrees, by the universe's very design and order. However, the willingness—the desire, in fact—of disbelievers and unbelievers to believe humanistic answers that are often based on the tiniest, and sometimes the flimsiest, shreds of evidence can be downright appalling.

Today, in intellectualism's heyday, despair is greater than ever. Humanity's problems only spiral downward. Depression is an epidemic. A fallen world only builds on its previous inventions of evil to produce more evil. Our education and knowledge makes some things better, but just as many things get worse. Every great society erodes from within due to evil that flourishes there. But, tragically, the blind continue to allow other blind people to lead them, while all claim to see.

Fallen humanity has a need to feel in control, to obtain and manage the knowledge of good and evil. It has been that way from the beginning of humankind. Humanism must prove a cause for this universe, other than that of the divine. To make a case for unbelief, humanistic science and philosophy must attempt to rationalize and demonstrate the impossible—that what we can presently study and observe was brought about by inorganic and organic processes that originated through random chance.

So, it is concluded here that, ultimately, unbelief is not, at its core, brought on by the logic of the mind but by the illogic of the heart because of humankind's fleshly desire to be "god" ourselves.

Unbelief is ultimately a heart problem because, as the prophet Jeremiah noted long ago, "The heart is deceitful above all things and beyond cure." Then, he asks those who might allow their hearts to be their guides and their gods, "Who can understand it?"[20]

The answer to the prophet's question is that no one but God can understand the human heart, that place within us where mind, body, soul, and spirit merge and interact. Because he made it, and God sees all that goes on within it. Therefore, for humankind, hearing and understanding the truth requires faith in the God who does understand our hearts as well as the rest of us. It requires the reasonable faith that is an intellectual, an emotional, and a spiritual recognition and admission of what is and what has always been.

In the beginning, God… And, in the end, God…

Inspiration: Science is not bad. It is good. Good science is, in fact, ultimately the original source for the study of theology. Simply put, science is the study of the physical, the stuff we are made of. Philosophy is not bad. It is good. It is simply the intellectual exploration of knowledge and existence. Thinking, wondering, and questioning are not bad. All new learning begins with speculation and exploration, hypothesizing and theorizing. Biblical faith is not contrary to science; in fact, it is the only thing that is consistent with it. Science is not—should not be, anyway—contrary to faith. Faith should not be contrary to science. Science, like everything else to do with humans, operates on faith. The basic building block of creation is not material in nature, that which can be seen only with the human eyes. The basic building block is seen only through the lens of faith itself. Faith is at the foundation of what it means to be human—we are made in the image of God. Unlike the other creatures, humankind—every one of us—breathes the most special breath of life—the breath of God himself. And, because of it, we have the opportunity to experience life to the full—life as God knows it!

But to experience the life of God, we must first believe in the God who can breathe new life into us.

Prayer: God, purify my heart that I might seek, find, and drink of pure truth. May my motives be honest, my search sincere, my thinking reasonable, my answers true, and my faith pure.

Reflection: What is the basis of my doubt? What is the basis of my faith? What do I honestly and sincerely believe? Why?

References:
1. Heb. 3:7–11.
2. Heb. 3:12–14.
3. Rom. 8:16.
4. Heb. 3:15–19.

5. Rom. 1:20.
6. Rom. 1:21–23.
7. 1 Cor. 1:18–21, 25.
8. Eph. 4:17–19.
9. Prov. 4:23.
10. Rom. 6:16.
11. John 20:26–28.
12. John 20:29.
13. Gen. 1:1.
14. Rev. 22:13.
15. Rom. 1:20.
16. Ps. 14:1.
17. Col. 1:16.
18. Heb. 1:3.
19. Robert Jastrow, as quoted by B. Durbin, "A Scientist Caught Between Two Faiths: Interview with Robert Jastrow," Christianity Today, Vol. 26, 6 August 1982, p. 15.
20. Jer. 17:9.

Other Books by Ronnie Worsham Available on Amazon.com

Discovering Jesus, A Self-Study Workbook
Forty Days on the Mountain with God
Fighting and Beating Depression
A Funny Little Cow Ponders Pain

44141010R00114

Made in the USA
San Bernardino, CA
08 January 2017